212°
THE
COMPLETE
TRADER

212° THE COMPLETE TRADER

A Unique Comprehension to Add That "Extra Degree"

GOD & ROHAN MEHTA

Notion Press

Old No. 38, New No. 6
McNichols Road, Chetpet
Chennai - 600 031

First Published by Notion Press 2017
Copyright © God & Rohan Mehta 2017
All Rights Reserved.

ISBN 978-1-946983-95-4

This book has been published with all reasonable efforts taken to make the material error-free after the consent of the author. No part of this book shall be used, reproduced in any manner whatsoever without written permission from the author, except in the case of brief quotations embodied in critical articles and reviews.

The Author of this book is solely responsible and liable for its content including but not limited to the views, representations, descriptions, statements, information, opinions and references ["Content"]. The Content of this book shall not constitute or be construed or deemed to reflect the opinion or expression of the Publisher or Editor. Neither the Publisher nor Editor endorse or approve the Content of this book or guarantee the reliability, accuracy or completeness of the Content published herein and do not make any representations or warranties of any kind, express or implied, including but not limited to the implied warranties of merchantability, fitness for a particular purpose. The Publisher and Editor shall not be liable whatsoever for any errors, omissions, whether such errors or omissions result from negligence, accident, or any other cause or claims for loss or damages of any kind, including without limitation, indirect or consequential loss or damage arising out of use, inability to use, or about the reliability, accuracy or sufficiency of the information contained in this book.

Contents

Disclaimer	vii
Acknowledgements	ix
Introduction	xi
What Is 212°: The Complete Trader All About	1
Be Ready to Become 212°: The Complete Trader!	5
Knowing Yourself – Survey	8
Chapter 1: Cold Water Shower Theory	11
Chapter 2: Trader vs. Investor	14
Chapter 3: The 5 Stages of a Trader's/Investor's Life	19
Chapter 4: A Happy Loss Manifesto	36
Chapter 5: Doing Things That Are DISLIKED	41
Chapter 6: The Don't Know Manifesto	46
Chapter 7: The Biggest Myth and the Biggest Boon	50
Chapter 8: 3 Types of Traders & A Master Formula to be the Wealthiest Trader/Investor	55
Chapter 9: The 4 Monkeys Approach	63
Chapter 10: The 3 Most Essential Hobbies of a Trader/Investor	71
Chapter 11: The 6 Key Reasons Why 90% of Traders/Investors Face Losses	76
Chapter 12: The 7 Most Important Questions to Ask before Taking a Trade	86
Chapter 13: The Bull, Bear and Pig Phases	94
Chapter 14: The 2 Best Tools for Trade & Investment	100
Chapter 15: 212° Investment Thesis	104
Chapter 16: Formula No. 21	113
Chapter 17: Magical Money Management	118

Chapter 18:	212° Trading/Investment Systems Designing	126
Chapter 19:	212° System Backtesting	133
Chapter 20:	The 3 Important C's for Trading/Investing	139
Chapter 21:	212° The Spiritual Trader	145
Chapter 22:	The Discipline Factor	167
Chapter 23:	10 Qualities to Trade Like Rama & Not Be a Ravana	182
Chapter 24:	The Day of a 212°: The Complete Trader	189
Chapter 25:	Traderpreneur – Trading as a Real Business	194
Chapter 26:	The EPW Model	203
Chapter 27:	12 Learnings for Being a 212° Trader/Investor	212
Chapter 28:	21 Things I Wished to Have Known before I Started Trading/Investing	219
Chapter 29:	The KIDS Approach	221

Disclaimer

Mr. Rohan Mehta is a Professionally Independent Trader & Investor; he is neither a SEBI Registered Investment Advisor nor a Research Analyst. The book is solely based on the experience of his trading and investing Journey. Though every bit of this book is followed and tested by Rohan, the readers should still ensure due diligence, before taking an Investment or a Trade; they should rather contact their Financial Advisors or Mentors. In some topics discussed in the book, Rohan's thought process might possibly be opposite to conventional theories of markets, but a reader must understand that everyone is different, and has his own niche in trading and investing. The Risk of loss in trading in Future Contracts, commodity, options, or equity investments can be substantial. Therefore, an investor should understand the risk involved in investing/trading and must assume responsibility for the risk associated with such investments/trades. One should carefully consider whether such trading is suitable for him in light of his circumstances and financial risk-taking ability.

Acknowledgements

I would like to acknowledge:

Almighty God, who is the Co-author of this book; the one who motivated me to write to the best of my knowledge and gave me this prime profession and wisdom of Investing and Trading.

My Grand Parents – my Grand Father who gave me an invaluable amount of 50,000 rupees to Invest in Stock Market, and the one who always believed in me when others failed to do so. My grandmother who always told me to strongly believe in God and to take a calculated risk in life.

My Parents and My Sister who were always there with me in my good as well as bad times.

My Wife Namrata and Adorable Daughter Vani for Supporting and Motivating Me to Achieve All of My Strenuous Goals and for Their Sacrifice of Family Time That Was Allotted to This Book.

Mr. Partha Shah who motivated me to enter the Stock Market Profession.

Mr. Hitesh Mali for accompanying me in the journey of learning and understanding the markets and being my mentor figure throughout.

Mr. Tejas Sarvaiya who has been an amazing support, more than a friend, a "Shifu" who advised me to explore research as a career, and now as a Trading & Investing Partner.

Mr. Vishvesh Chauhan who suggested me to read Michael Covel's *Trend Following* and the one who showcased me Trend Following Systems.

Mr. Bharat Sadrani who encouraged me to learn technical aspects and apply them in assessing markets. Special thanks to his Creation of Bazaar Indicator Software that has been a key tool in enhancing my skills as a Trader and Investor.

Mrs. Jigna Patel, Mrs. Vibhati Gandhi and Mr. Hardik Gandhi along with the Whole Turtle Team for being colleagues with an exceptional value and support system.

Mr. Chirag Shah and the Full Jainam Family who motivated me to keep reading as a hobby and taught me principles of life.

Ms. Ajita Parekh for helping me in publishing the book.

Mr. Joel Osteen – My Spiritual Mentor, who made me believe in God!

I am grateful to great traders and investors *Mr. Rakesh Jhunjhunwala, Mr. Utpal Sheth, Mr. Radhakrishnan Damani, Mr. Atul Suri, Mr. Ed Seykota, Mr. Michael Covel, Mr. Paul Tudor Jones, late Mr. Jessie Livermore, Mr. Warren Buffett, Mr. Charlie Munger, Mr. Carl Icahn* and many more for being a recurrent inspiration.

Special Acknowledgement to you for buying the book and supporting me in my purpose, which has now turned into *our* purpose.

Introduction

Namaste!

I was Born in Bhavnagar, Gujarat, to a middle-class family where education is considered as an essential requirement for getting a good job. However, throughout my academic life, I had always been an average student, till I discovered the passion for markets – in fact, every Indian Gujarati Baniya inherently holds it in his blood. I started my professional career as an Investor more than a decade ago, taking a loan amounting to Rs 50,000 from my father, which rather my grandfather had forced him to lend. Eventually, I immersed all the lent money in trading like an amateur Trader. From that day onwards, the urge for returning the borrowed money and understanding the mode of making money from the stock market had commenced.

To be honest, during the childhood, no one aspires to be a "Professional Trader or an Investor" as all the successful traders or investors I have encountered, entered the market by chance and not by choice/plan.

The irony turned out to be **"A dumb fellow entered the arena and made the intelligent fellows work under him."**

During the early phase of my career, I had tried my hands in all the possible avenues in the stock market, such as a technical trader, fundamental investor, news trader and speculator. However, I failed to outshine anywhere. Then, one fine day, while conversing with my friend

Mr. Vishvesh, a Fund Manager in a leading brokerage house, I shared my desire to explore the techniques for trading and he suggested me to read *Trend Following* by Mr. Michael Covel and it changed my life forever.

While reading the book, I extracted numerous interesting logic and techniques for being a trader/investor and a trend follower. Moreover, this book had lent me a curiosity to read more and more to gain knowledge and evolve. In today's date, I have read almost every book available on Amazon in the areas of trend following, traders' psychology, discipline, money management, biographies and market wizards etc. Thus, this book is a blend of all the gathered thoughts of the great authors that inspired me to be a *212°: The Complete Trader* as well as my inferences drawn from real-time trading.

During those days, I was working as a Research Head at a stockbroking company in Gujarat, India and I believed that trading through systems is very easy and I recommended trading to everyone, but no one could hold on to the profits and cut down the losses. Thereafter, I finally concluded that trading is not everyone's cup of tea and those who are willing to be a trader must gain a deliberate understanding of trading and be a professional trader within. I mentored and trained more than 5,000 traders and in this process, I thought of writing a book to introduce my major deductions from the journey of me being a *212°: The Complete Trader* to the whole world.

When I thought of writing the book, 2 diverse thoughts were running in my head – "Should I write a book? Or flourish in my career in a manner that a book is written on me instead?"

After a lot of thought process, I finally concluded to write a book, as I did not want any other Rohan to lose his valuable money as an amateur trader; he should rather understand the real process of being a *212°: The Complete Trader*.

Today I am the co-founder of Turtle Wealth, Professional Trader, Investor, and a disciplined mentor. At the age of 32, I am **"Financially Abundant"** and that is the only possibility of being a *212°* Trader & Investor. I have a purpose of promoting #Tradingasabusiness across the globe. I am sure this book will take you on an amazing journey of being the Trader/an Investor that one had always desired to be.

"Writing is a way of talking without being interrupted."
Jules Renard

Regards,

Rohan Mehta

What Is 212°: The Complete Trader All About

In the Journey of reading books, I encountered the book written by Sam Parker - *212° The Extra Degree* and I loved the concept and thought of implementing this idea in keeping the Title of my Book - *212°: The Complete Trader*.

What is 212°?

"Till 211 degrees, water is hot and after reaching 212°, it starts boiling. And with boiling water, comes steam, and with steam, you can empower even a train! Thus, it takes just one extra degree to make all the difference (Parker, 2005)." Through this book, one will gain that 1 Extra Degree or element which will make him the best trader or investor.

In life, that one extra degree only makes the difference between the winners and losers, successful and unsuccessful, rich and wealthy, and that one degree only holds the power of changing the virtue of our life.

When we think of Trading and Investing, we believe that the technique, tools, and numbers are only important, while in reality, we are still incomplete. To be wholesome, we are required to have that extra degree. This is the main essence of the book; each chapter is crafted in a manner that it helps you evolve and develop that extra degree in you.

Trading is also similar to playing sports, being a Zen Monk or riding a roller coaster. So, what is that one extra degree that will make you the complete trader?

It includes:

- Mastering Winner mindset
- Mastering Discipline & Emotional Quotient
- Mastering Trading/Investing Techniques
- Mastering Money Management
- Mastering own self and much more...

The Complete Trader is not the one who is Rich but one who is wealthy,

Not the one who must work for Money, but the one whose money works for him,

Not the one who sacrifices everything to earn money, but the one who has everything and still works for increasing the wealth.

This is the Journey from being Incomplete to a Complete Trader/Investor.

How to Read This Book

It is essential to read the book step by step, yet one may start from any chapter one prefers to; he would still be able to connect with all the other chapters of the book very well.

There are certain Questions & Exercises that are important to know yourself better and decide on the actions you need to take. The practical implication of the knowledge bestowed through this book is significant, as the main purpose of the book would only be fulfilled if the real-life implication of the shared knowledge is ensured.

Every chapter will be followed by:

- Summary & Learnings from the chapter
- 3 Action Steps you would take after reading the chapter
- Date of completion of each Action
- Accountable person: The one who would be accountable for observing your actions and achievements

It is advisable that you complete all the action points in each chapter and then proceed to the next chapter. There will be different steps for different structures and topics; it is important to follow all the instructions rigorously for getting the best results.

The Objective of the Book

The clear objective of the book is to make the readers $212°$: *The Complete Traders* and imbibe that 1 extra Degree in them to achieve Nirvana in Trading/investing.

To give the readers a new opportunity of pursuing Trading/Investing as a business that could make incredible returns and assist them in balancing the work life in a manner that sufficient time could be devoted to family, health, hobbies, and life.

What not to Expect from this Book

- That someone will read the book for you and summarize it for you to simply implement; rather, you must read and implement everything yourself.

- Holy Grail Trading System that will make you super rich instantly
- Multi-bagger Stock Recommendations
- Short and easy success formula to make you a great trader/Investor
- My Personal Trading/Investing Systems
- Anything which has instant gratification module to please your desires
- Any Guarantee or warranty; it will serve as only the genuine knowledge and wisdom to make you a world-class Trader/Investor

What Would Be Exceptional About This Book

- Simple Language to understand the real secret of being the best Trader/Investor
- Everything that I have written is based on my experience and I have followed it throughout my life
- Life-Changing Experiences
- Great Exercises and real examples

Be Ready to Become 212°: The Complete Trader!

What is Trading

Let us understand the Real Meaning of Trading.

In ancient times, trading used to take place with the barter system, where one could exchange goods against goods, and in today's date, goods are exchanged against currency and vice versa.

The General meaning of trading is buying and selling of a product, service or commodity. Be it in any business, trading will be involved; ranging from Walmart to a Fruit Seller, everyone trades; the difference is only in the way their trades are executed.

When one person/party purchases a good and sells it to other person/party with a profit margin, it is simply known as Trading. This is the basic business characteristic; that is right! But in the stock market as well, there exist purchasers and sellers, and thereby, trade is executed in the stock market. Though the duration of keeping or holding the goods (Stocks) differs from a day, a week or a month to a year or even more than that.

Trade is the life and the economy of the world. The 2 fundamental reasons that lead to trading are:

- Buyer & Seller
- Demand & Supply

Both the reasons are prevalent in stock markets as well. The trading of securities in the stock market is not considered to be a well-versed profession, while in my opinion, trading is a profession that is as holy as any other renowned business/profession in the world.

Trading is generally considered to be a bad word and is misconceived with speculation and speculators, while Investment is accepted as a good word. However, if we see the dictionary meaning of both the terms, the basic essence remains the same, i.e., both involve the process of buying and selling something; the only difference is in the form of holding period and the applied approach. **"Trading is more of a science and Investing is more of an art."** Mr. George Soros is a Trader and Mr. Warren Buffett is an Investor, and both are equally successful and wealthy in their respective careers. During my initial stage of the career, I used to ask my seniors about the better choice between Trading and Investing. Many preferred Trading; while some suggested Investing; I understood everyone holds his individual choice and I eventually decided to be both, as *"the religion in the market is to make money, irrespective of being a trader or an investor."* Thus, I decided to be both Trader and Investor and have made money at both the ends. While Speaking of a *212°: The Complete Trader*, I am not referring to an intraday trader or a speculator; it is a wholesome phenomenon that is inclusive of all – Trader, Investor, Fund Manager, Day Trader, Positional Trader, Long-Term Trader, Value Investor, Contrarian, Growth Investor, Hedger and even Arbitrageur.

As, when the term Trading comes, it always means Investments; to make it simple, it is just the way the Money is created. Thus, this book is not restricted to only trading, it is also associated with any of the above-mentioned role one plays in the market.

Knowing Yourself – Survey

"Trading is a Quest of knowing oneself."

Let's take a swift check on where one stands today. One needs to answer either Yes or No to the following Questions – be honest with yourself. These 10 Questions will tell you where you stand today.

Survey – know Yourself		
Questions to Understand You! (Please tick Yes/No)		
Questions	Yes	No
1. Are you stress-free while trading and investing? Do you get good sleep without worrying about the market?		
2. Are you flexible enough to take any of the side positions – either long or short – as per the market trend?		
3. Do you often find that the market trends are in your favour?		
4. Has your trading or Investing portfolio given more than 30% return in the last 12 months?		
5. Do you possess any method or system for trading or investing that states exactly when you shall enter or exit the trade?		

6. Do you cut your losses quickly and hold profits till the time trend ends?		
7. Is your risk (stop loss) predefined while entering a trade?		
8. Do you understand Leverage and money management rule in your trading and investing?		
9. Do you have a goal? How much money do you intend to earn in the next 1, 2, 5 or 10 years?		
10. Do you have a mentor who guides you while taking trading and investing decisions?		

Result: No. of YES -_____, NO -_____

If you scored more than 7 Nos: You fall under the zone of recommended reading of this book and to follow the suggested principles with an immediate effect under the guidance of a professional mentor. There could be a case of you being in a dilemma to leave or stay in the Stock Market. Moreover, there could also be a possibility of missing link – either in your knowledge or otherwise – which hinders you from outperforming. Such missing links will be resolved by attaining a thorough understanding of *212°: The Complete Trader* and it would make you score 10 Yeses eventually.

If you scored more than 3 Yeses & less than 8 Nos: You fall in a zone of being on the right track of progress and knowledge. Although, there is the lack of discipline, money management, longevity and the right approach. However, you can score all 10 yeses; therefore, this book will take you towards a journey of building the best in you.

"My Commitment is to ensure that, after reading this book completely, the answer to all 10 Questions should be YES."

Chapter 1

Cold Water Shower Theory

"All the Success is found beyond the comfort zone."

As humans, we are likely to be comfortable and stay in our comfort zone, but the irony of life states that no success could be achieved while staying in it. We have to move out of it and bear some hardships in order to achieve our goals, i.e., the state of being in a relatively more comfortable state of life.

Cold Water theory would be an appropriate description of the above-stated philosophy. It states that all of us like to take a bath with hot or warm water, while bathing with cold water is disliked by the majority. My daughter is very afraid of it and dislikes it just like anybody else. It is hated because it makes us uncomfortable. However, it is a well-known fact that taking shower in the cold water keeps an individual fresh, attentive and productive all day long. Yet, one fails to choose the cold water shower above his comfort level.

Cold Water Theory encourages us to step out of our **Comfort Zone** to ensure adequate focus and time management. Post waking up early in morning, the first thing one should do is to have a Cold Water Shower. I assure you that – such a day would be the most productive day.

I understood and realized the significance of this theory when I took the decision of leaving my Job – a reputed position with a handsomely paid salary for being a full-time trader/Investor. I took one year to approach my boss and execute my desire as I found it as hard as taking a cold water shower. The phase of conversion from a comfort zone to the one which is uncomfortable – but fruitful in the long run – is the matter of only a few seconds. However, after having taken the stand, the attained inner peace and satisfaction level is beyond imagination.

A similar rule applies to trading/investing: one doesn't like to read and learn but to directly enter the game and learn in his own way. Cold Water Shower theory suggests one to do the uncomfortable thing in Stock Markets – to be Comfortable in future – and even while reading this book, there could be some actions or conducts suggested in this book that might make you uncomfortable with the practical implication, but in the end, if adopted adequately, they would certainly give you positive results and growth in future.

I often tell myself and to others: ***"To be comfortable in life, we need to undergo uncomfortable things first."***

Before beginning with the book, I would like to share a secret with you that to be the best in trading & investing: ***"Start doing the uncomfortable things."***

Summary and Learnings:

- Take Cold Water Showers – do the uncomfortable things first
- It takes few seconds to be comfortable in doing the Uncomfortable thing
- In Stock Markets, learning from books or taking training is similar to taking "A Cold Shower"

3 Action Steps to be taken from this Chapter:

1. Action Steps:

_____

_____

Date to Achieve it: _____

Accountable Person: _____

2. Action Steps:

_____

_____

Date to Achieve it: _____

Accountable Person: _____

3. Action Steps:

_____

_____

Date to Achieve it: _____

Accountable Person: _____

Notes:

_____
_____
_____
_____
_____
_____
_____
_____

Chapter 2

Trader vs. Investor

"90% Individuals are Investors by Force, not by WILL."

There is a never-ending debate about who is better among the investors and the traders? To follow the 212° Approach, one should hold the characteristics of both investors and traders. In this section of the book, one will explore the trick of compounding his wealth, while being a trader and investor and holding different mindsets while Trading and Investing. After 10 Years of Research and practice, we have found how to be both and to exploit the opportunities both as a trader as well as the investor.

One thing to be understood is ***"No one wins over the other; both are remarkable in their own way. If we extract the positive features of both and implement them, it can prove to be one of the best mixes in the Market."***

An Investor is someone like Mr. Warren Buffett who buys a business and talks for centuries; trader is someone like Mr. George Soros or Mr. Jessie Livermore who focuses on prices and trades in different timeframes, doing long and short.

"Fundamentals suggest what to buy or short, while technical suggest when to do it."

Investors generally watch the value in a stock with R.O.E, R.O.C.E., P.E., E.P.S., B.V. etc., whereas, traders watch price, direction, and trend. The intention of both is to earn money but their modes of earning are different. Thus, where to trade and where to invest? This is the biggest question on the earth that will be simplified here.

"Trading is something which is highly liquid and popular, while investing is boring and less popular."

One would have observed that the world's best traders generally trade in index futures, commodities, currencies and highly liquid stocks which are more cyclical in both nature and business.

Whereas, looking at the best investors: they invest in the companies which are more of consumable stocks with great cash flow and the products that people can't live without, pertaining to zero debt – companies like Apple, Coke, P&G, Gillette, Bosch, Colgate etc.

As a $212°$: *The complete Trader*, one needs to develop 2 sides of the mind, the first side would think as the best trader and the other as a boring Investor.

We believe trading certainly leads to a cash flow, wherein one can generate money in the most liquid form by being in both long and short positions. For instance, if one has a business where he is able to create cash flow and then he shifts that money into buying good quality stock or investing in MF (Mutual funds) or ETF (Exchange Traded funds). Similar is the case with a trader, who doesn't have any other business, as his cash flow is generated through trading itself, thus, whatever is created from trading, one can invest in quality stocks.

A trader cannot make it big without having a correct investing approach and an investor will have hurdles in staying invested for a longer period if the needed cash flow is not generated.

10 Comparisons between Traders and Investors

Trader	Investor
1. Trader Trades with Price	1. Investor Invests in business figures
2. Trader's Funda - **"Buy on High, Sell on Low"**	2. Investor's Funda - **"Buy Right, Sit Tight"**
3. Trade in cyclical, highly liquid assets which are also popular	3. Invest in boring, defensive, cash flow making business, which is yet to be popular
4. Time: Till the trend ends	4. Long-Term – and I literally mean for *long term*
5. Averaging of Losses is a sin	5. Averaging of losses is allowed if they are pre-planned
6. Requires high level of skills, discipline and money management	6. Requires high level of patience and conviction
7. Cannot survive without taking Short positions	7. Can survive by only taking long positions
8. The Decision is taken majorly from the mind	8. The Decision should be a mix of both the heart and the mind
9. Fast in booking losses, slow in booking profits	9. Slow in booking losses as well as Profits
10. Cannot invest in what he trades	10. Cannot trade in what he Invests

A few years ago, we used to play music cassettes which had A & B Sides, likewise, *212°: The Complete Trader* has 2 sides of the mind: as a trader and as an investor, and that is how one can be *212°: The Complete Trader*.

Summary & Learnings:

- Trading is more of Science, and Investing is an Art
- Trader focuses on Prices, whereas Investor focuses on Value
- Trader and Investor both share the same motive of earning money; just the style of earning differs
- It's Important to have 2 sides of mind – as a Trader & an Investor

3 Action Steps to be taken from this Chapter:

1. Action Steps:

_____

_____

Date to Achieve it: _____

Accountable Person: _____

2. Action Steps:

_____

_____

Date to Achieve it: _____

Accountable Person: _____

3. Action Steps:

_____

_____

Date to Achieve it: _____

Accountable Person: _____

Notes:

_____

_____

_____

_____

_____

_____

_____

_____

Chapter 3

The 5 Stages of a Trader's/Investor's Life

Being a *212°: The complete Trader* is like playing a video game, wherein you are supposed to pass different stages. As you pass the stages, your maturity level increases, and the desperation to win and gain increases time to time. The different stages of a trader's life have hardly been mentioned in any of the academic records in the history, thus, I hereby introduce you to different stages of a Trader's or Investor's life.

1st Stage: Amateur Desire

"If we enter the Stock market with a lot of Money and No Experience, we will end up with Lots of Experience and Probably no Money."

This is an initial stage, wherein one tries his hands in stock trading because of having heard of it as an easy mode of earning money – however, this is simply not the case. Moreover, in the stock markets, there are no entry barriers – any adult can open an account and begin trading even with the modest amount of 1,000 INR in hand. At the initial stage, one also gets carried away with the success stories of legends such as Mr. Rakesh Jhunjhunwala, Mr. Warren Buffett, Mr. George Soros, etc. Thus, he begins investing with a high hope of making huge profits; rest we all know what happens. This stage could be further diversified into 3 steps:

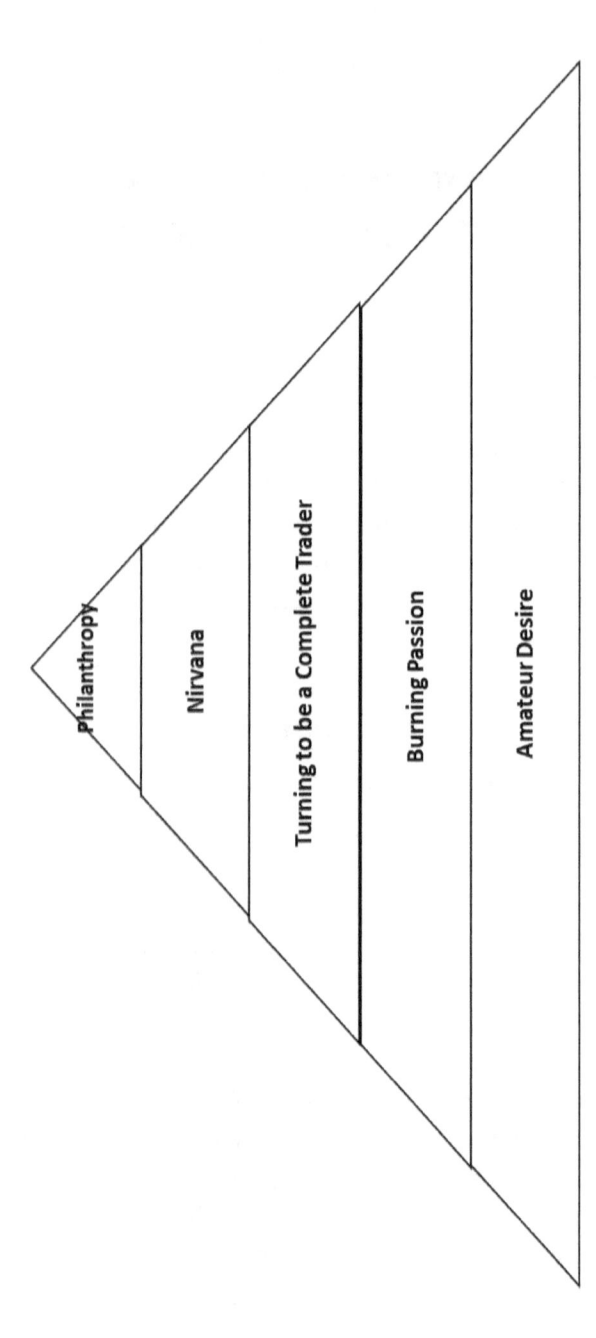

1st: Desire – It's the desire of earning huge amount of money or making a second source of income or beating the markets with the possessed knowledge that makes us attracted to the stock market. Without any desire, it is impossible for anyone to enter any business, but in trading, the desire is only associated with making a lot of money without putting hard work; that desire takes us through different steps and stages.

2nd: Initial Experience – After the desire, we have an initial experience of opening an account, as per a survey, 90% of the accounts are opened for IPO (Initial Public Offering) and with a thought process of investing in good Companies, but focus changes to **"Get Rich Quick"** formula. Thereafter, Investor starts trading blindly without any knowledge and wisdom or by seeking advice from the people – mostly brokers – who might not have made profits even in a single YOY (Year on Year) and would only target his/ her commission or brokerages. Such an initial experience is also taken by individuals from doing the job or undergoing training for understanding the markets and its nature. This, however, is the more idealistic way in comparison to directly opening an account and starting the process of Trading/Investing.

3rd: Doing General Mistakes – Once we enter into the world of numbers, we, as humans, hold a tendency of committing **"Initial Instinct Mistakes"** such as:

- Starting as an Investor, eventually turning into a trader
- Over Trading, Over Leverage
- Listening to Dealer/Broker who is interested only in his commission/brokerage
- Seeking thousands of Tips & Advice
- Keeping a constant track of prices
- Anxiety

- Investing in Good time, taking an exit in the worst time
- No plan of an exit point
- Exiting too soon in Profit; holding on to the loss positions until late

Thereafter, one fine day, either the broker will ask the investor to sell the stock or holding, or out of frustration/anxiety, the holder himself would sell the holding and start a new game called **"Blame Game"** where he begins blaming everything in the world, referring to:

- Economy
- Brokers & Dealers
- Markets
- Destiny, luck etc.

"A man can fail many times, but he is not a failure until he begins to blame somebody else." – John Burroughs

We start criticizing this mode of investment as the worst across the globe, without realizing that the fault lies with us. It is because of our lack of skills and knowledge that we had to bear such losses.

In this 1st Stage, ***80% of the Investors or Traders are likely to detach themselves from trading/investing forever and only 20% of them would proceed to the second stage.***

2nd Stage: Burning Passion

It is the most interesting stage; it's the stage where only a few amateur investors reach after reviewing their past mistakes as they try learning the rules of the game rather than playing it blindly. I have gone through this stage; this stage is very stressful and troublesome, but it is a very crucial stage to make an individual understand the real mechanism of the markets.

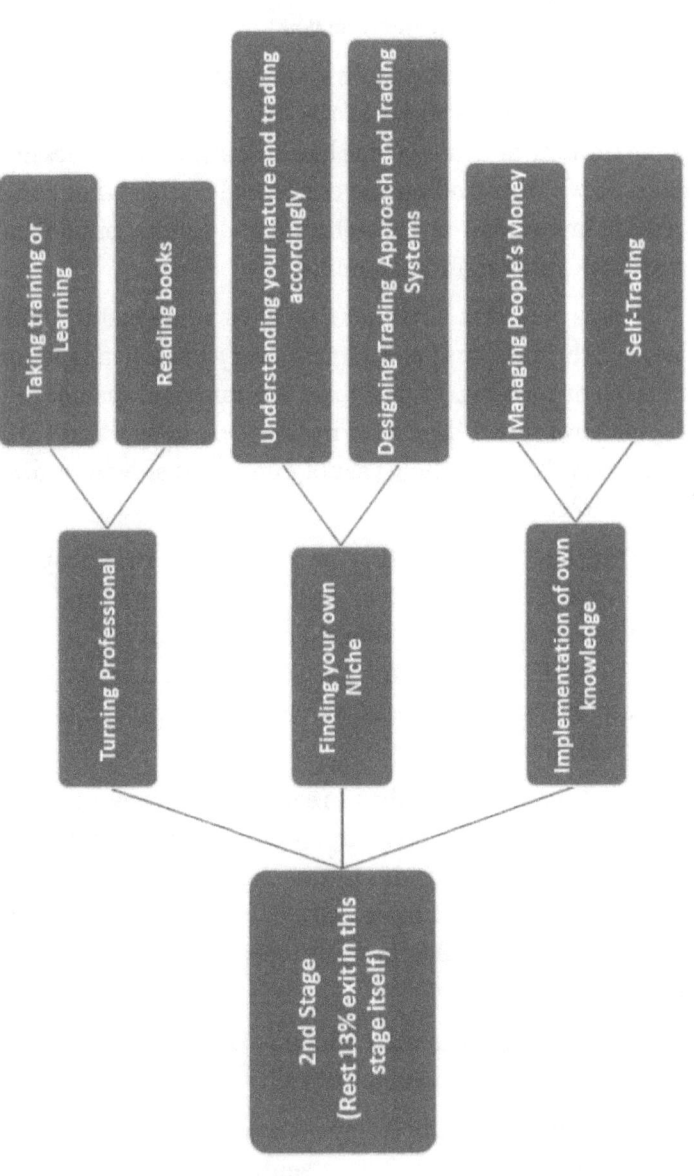

1ˢᵗ: Turning Professional – *"If you don't take the market seriously, the market won't take you seriously either."*

We understand that trading and Investing is not as easy as we considered it to be in the first stage as it demands some training and knowledge like how any other profession does, so we start finding the concerned courses that could provide knowledge on the technical and fundamental front with basic market understanding.

I was not that fortunate to have someone to guide me, which made me read almost every book available on 4shared or torrents. At that time, e-commerce was not that popular in India. I have read nearly 900+ books, and I still remember that one whole year of mine went only in reading those books.

Trading and Investing was popular in European and American Countries, and thus, books on such topics were easily available there. While, in India, such level of skills and success in trading was hard to find, consequently, a narrowed range of Indian books was available for access.

The first ever book that I read on Markets was *"Trend Following by Michael Covel,"* and it played a huge role in my inclination towards trading, and thereafter, my learning through books turned to be a never-ending process. Owing to this habit, I was able to train more than 15,000 Traders and Investors till now.

2ⁿᵈ: Finding your own Niche – "Trading is all about discovering your own Personality."

After having attained some knowledge through books and practical learning, it is essential to relate it to our

Personality and our core objectives. Through this exercise, I learned that High-Frequency Trading never suited my personality as I am a medium-term to a long-term type of a trader, therefore, I began to design systems that could suit my lifestyle and nature and it worked for me.

I was never comfortable with systems that held more than 4 trades in a month and I never preferred sticking to the screens, thus I designed systems which were more on an EOD (End of the Day) basis.

Therefore, it is not necessary that the world's best system would turn out to be best for us as well; it rather depends on our inner instinct. For e.g., I am a Jain – Vegan – and I went to a gala dinner in the USA where a chef had made the world's best non- vegetarian dish; it could be the best, but not for me. Similar is the case with trading; there are numerous ways through which trading can be done, but only that mode of trading should be selected which suits our personality and instincts. Moreover, we need to understand that making the suitable trading systems alone does not suffice; an adequate understanding of money management, discipline and psychology is also equally important for making money through trading/investing.

3rd Step: Implementation of Knowledge – It is hard to ask a trader to restrict his pace of trading at this stage and wait for the correct time, because, one becomes totally confident regarding knowledge of the market. Thus, there could be 2 ideal options through which trading could be executed and attained knowledge could be implemented:

1. **To Manage Someone else's money:** Many Traders don't have an initial investment to Trade or invest

in, so they arrange others' money to invest, for instance, family members or any investors who have money but do not have time or knowledge to manage their funds.
2. **Self-Trader:** If a trader has an initial investment, he will start investing a smaller portion of his savings or earnings in the market.

Considering all the stages, yet some tough times could be faced where **"Patience, Persistence and Perspiration"** will be tested in different forms, owing to unsupportive market conditions, internal greed or fear, lack of discipline and emotions. Thus, due to such circumstances, *13% of the 20% traders get filtered after the first stage and give up to start searching new avenues to earn money.*

3rd Stage: Turning to be "The Complete Trader"

Welcome to the Professional Trader League. If one enters this stage, it means he has surpassed all the hurdles of the second stage and has started experiencing the real magic of the market. Once this stage is reached by a person, all basic amenities in life that one aspires to achieve, such as a good house, an office, and other basic luxuries are attained. But he does not settle with the basic facilities, and he rather strives for MORE. There are 3 Steps of being **"The Complete Trader."**

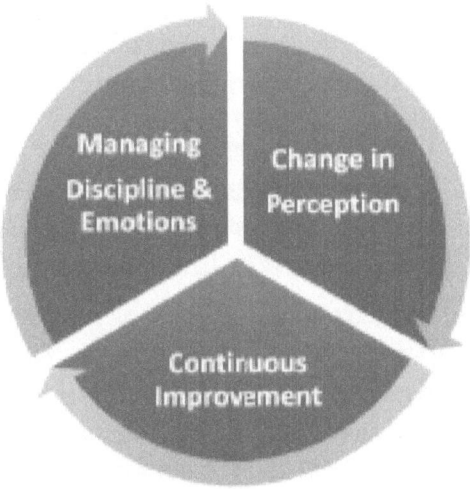

1st: Managing Discipline and Emotions – In the second stage, money, and strategy are the focus areas, but when you enter the third stage, you will find that strategy, charts or systems holds only 10–15% of the total stake, while the rest of the stake is held by discipline. I remember I read almost all the available books on discipline. One can't be disciplined in trading if he is not disciplined in regular life. Trust me, in the third stage, the key is to fight with our own selves and go ahead. I still hold regrets for having missed some lucrative trades because of poor discipline in my real life – How to remain disciplined has been discussed in the Discipline trader chapter.

In 1st Step, it's all about: Aspiring to earn money

2nd Step: Learning to Earn Money

3rd Step: Risk & Emotional Management

After entering the 3rd *Step*, one attempts to find the mode of securing discipline and controlling inner emotions that force an individual to:

- Take Early Profits
- Not to take a trade, as the market looks bad or good
- Buy Less Quantity or more Quantity
- Think it's an occasion; let's not trade

Believe me, *"The Trades that you missed, were the Greatest Trades."* The Trader in the third Stage understands himself better and sticks to the rules he had made.

2nd: Change in Perception – When anyone comes into the arena of trading, he comes with a **"Quick Rich"** thought process, but once he enters the third stage, he understands that "Quick Rich" manifesto is just a myth. As we enlarge our vision to have bigger trend trades, rather than going for High-Frequency Trading, or let me put in this way – when we enter, we believe "it's all about money," but later, we understand it's about following the rules and then **"Turning them bigger."** Like every trader, my trading perception at the initial stage was to make a lot of money; today it has completely shifted to remaining 100% disciplined in executing trades and sticking to my rules. Now, if I do this, I have 50% Probability of making money, but if I don't do it, I do not have even 1% probability.

Perception of trading changes in every stage, it will change a lot in 4th and 5th stages as well.

3rd: Continuous Improvement – *"Traders who just work for being better and better are the ones who grow bigger and bigger."* Improvement comes in different forms and ways.

"Market gives an opportunity to do mistakes every day, but not the repeated ones. If you do the same mistakes every day, it takes a very high tuition fee."

Till date, I have made almost 500 Trading & Investing Systems with continuous improvement in my thought process. With the passage of time, I aim at making simpler systems which are easy to understand and are easy to execute, so where does this wisdom come from?

It is a two-way street – you either meet wizards or read about them; I did both. I have met Mr. Ed Seykota, Mr. Warren Buffett, Mr. Charlie Munger, Mr. Samir Arora, Mr. Utpal Sheth, Mr. Rakesh Jhunjhunwala and many others and I have read almost 900+ Books and made continuous improvement in myself. Every day I think of making a system and I assure back testing all those systems manually.

As it is common for all types of businesses, the business could perish if regular improvement is not done; similar is the case with Trading/Investing. The short-term systems, which I trade, has been updated 5 times in the last 7 years to make them relatively smoother, less volatile and sharper with fewer drawdowns, without having changed their essence i.e., *"Larger Profits, Smaller Losses."*

4th Stage: Finding Nirvana

This is an incredible stage, where one is ahead in the 10% Squad, is making money, is happy and loving his work. Most importantly one is **"Financially Free."** It takes many years to enter such a stage, but once entered, it is surely a Nirvana!

I have divided this stage into 4 parts:

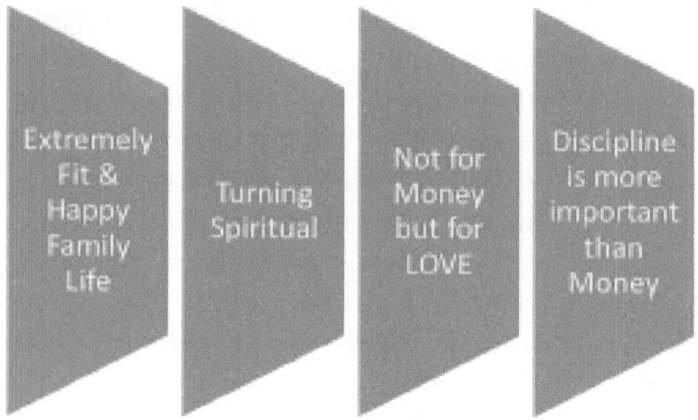

Phase 1: Extremely Fit and Happy Family Life – For a Trader/Investor, it is very important to be physically fit. If he is not, it brings a lot of fatigue, low energy and extremely less decisive power in him. No wonder why personnel from the army, air force, and navy are turning full-time traders. They have built discipline in themselves concerning to their health and execution of work.

In this stage, you start believing that health and happy family life hold a high priority as well, as ***"Health and Family are the backbone of a Trader for a long-term success."***

I give 120 minutes to health every day and sufficient quality time with family when I return from **"Enjoyment"** – I don't consider Trading/investing as work; it is, rather, enjoyment for me.

It is very important to pray to God, take blessing from parents, kiss spouse and hug kids when one leaves home for enjoyment. The energy held in such petty activities is beyond the description, as they hold the power of leading one to attain success for sure. If it is hard to believe that doing the above-stated activities could bring a positive change in your working style, try doing the reverse – fight and leave for office for a week and the difference will be evident.

Phase 2: Turning Spiritual – This is astonishing. In this stage, the trader surpasses the trading books and rather develops an interest in exploring religion through Bhagwad Gita, Upanishads, The Holy Bible, Quran, etc. and starts holding a divine connection with the God. Thus, the trader believes that adhering to the system is the only thing that is held in his hands; the result, however, rests with the God or Universe. The reality of the world is understood, and he inclines more towards "Doing the Right things over doing Good things."

I have read The Holy Bible; I hear the Podcast of Joel Osteen – the man who has given a new life to me – every day in the quest for reading Bhagwad Gita and my total view of trading and investing has changed and has reached a different level altogether, which could not be explained in words.

Phase 3: Not for Money, but for Love – Till Stage 3, it was completely restricted to money and its multiplication, but in Stage 4, it is not only about money – it is much beyond that.

The focus shifts from making money to loving the process, day by day, and enjoying the journey. We can say in this stage, that money comes as a by-product, as the major challenges as a trader have already been surpassed and Nirvana is a stage where it's a complete bliss and divine in place.

Many of you, after reading about this phase, would be thinking that if the money is not the focus, then the returns would decline, the answer is a big NO; returns would accelerate even more. This is because once your focus shifts from making money to enjoying the process and becoming a complete Nirvana Trader, your profits and wealth will spike up to a level beyond an individual's expectation.

Phase 4: Discipline is more important than Money – This is the stage where I would categorize myself in today's date. Moreover, I would encourage every reader to come into this stage as soon as possible.

"When Discipline weighs much more than making Money, you are a Trader Pal."

My office is centrally located with high traffic. When we leave the building, there are generally 2 ways to go back home – one is to go by the right side and another one is to go through the wrong side – yes, in India, we drive in the wrong sides too. The right side has a very long U-turn with 2 traffic signals, a lot of traffic, waste of time and waste of fuel, while taking the wrong route, it is the shortcut and holds no waste of time, fuel, and there are absolutely no signals.

So, what do the majority people do? No prize for guessing; 95% of the population takes the wrong route and only 5% of the people take the Long U-turn, sacrifice the fuel, time and energy, only because the most important thing for them is to follow the rules as they view the long run aspect of it.

No wonders the success ratio of traders in the world is not more than 5% as well, as rest of the people opt for a Shortcut-**"Quick Rich Formula."** Despite all the pains, when you start believing that discipline is more important than making money, that is the day you will achieve Nirvana!

5th Stage: Philanthropy - Giving Back

Zone of Financial Abundance: until the day I had met Mr. Warren Buffett, there was never a 5th Stage, but I understood the power of giving back. It is the law of Nature: **"What you give, is what you get in return;"** no wonder these legendary traders and investors are philanthropists.

I had studied about nearly 100 Billionaires in Forbes, and the most common characteristic among them was their custom of philanthropy, so why is it so that everyone who is wealthy – not just rich – is the philanthropist?

This is one of the most profound stages for an amateur, though not practical, as for why would anyone give something that is hard-earned, that has been invested for so many years to somebody else? However, once an individual realizes that he has achieved almost everything he desired, he would receive an inner call for giving back to the universe/ world/ society what has been earned from it.

One must decide the proportion of his earning he would prefer for donating every year. Along with this, one is also required to decide what would be his donating amount 10 years down the line. One with a limited income thinks of donating later when he would be earning well, but the fact is, if you cannot donate 1 rupee now, you won't be able to donate 100 rupees tomorrow, hence, start donating today as the secret of donating states that:

"The Faster you give, the faster it comes back to you – doubled."

In 130 crore of Population, nearly 129 crore people are the receivers and probably only 1 crore people could be counted under givers. Such people hold the potential of having that one extra degree; this zone is also called as the zone of **"Nirvana,"** achievement of being *212°: The Real Complete Trader.*

Summary & Learnings:

- All the Traders & Investors go through 5 different stages
- One has to figure out which stage he is currently standing at
- When discipline weighs more than the desire for earning money, that is the time when one proceeds towards gaining that extra degree
- Giving back is when you have achieved that one extra degree.

3 Action Steps to be taken from this Chapter:

Biggest Question – What would you do to get promoted to the next stage?

1. Action Steps:

_____

_____

Date to Achieve it: _____

Accountable Person: _____

2. Action Steps:

_____

_____

Date to Achieve it: _____

Accountable Person: _____

3. Action Steps:

_____

_____

Date to Achieve it: _____

Accountable Person: _____

Notes:

_____
_____
_____
_____
_____
_____
_____
_____
_____

Chapter 4

A Happy Loss Manifesto

"Trading is the Place where we enter only to earn Profits without any losses; the irony is that it never happens."

As one of the Great Traders has quoted, **"Profit takes care of itself; losses never do."**

The very first wisdom I got as a trader was **"Cut your Losses"** and I have seen over the period that this was the reason I have survived more than 10 years as a Trader/Investor, and it is also the same reason why people – who are not able to survive as a Trader or Investor – are not able to understand the Happy Loss Manifesto.

Generally, the term used for cutting the losses is keeping the **"Stop Loss"** – a commonly-heard phrase among traders, but very few follow it religiously – and with discipline – as no one likes to take loss, though the truth is, if the loss is not taken, it will be accompanied by numerous other losses and would lead to any of these scenarios:

1. Loss can widen more and more
2. New opportunities are not explored
3. A lot of time and energy is wasted to cover those losses

Let me put this with an Example: I had bought an XYZ Share at 100 rupees with my stop loss at 97 – 3% risk trade – of course with an expectation of a rise in price. The Market is volatile and has 50–50% probability that it may go up or go down.

The next day, it rose to 104, I did nothing; the following day it came down to 98 again, I did nothing, and the third day, it came down to 97 and I exited. After a few days, the stock was around 80 rupees, so such loss incurred by me is to be stated as my good loss or bad loss?

As at Turtle Wealth, we call Stop Loss as **"Happy Loss"** – a loss which we are happy to take, because if we don't take this loss, it will exceed, and we will lose even more – we define it to be a happy emotion rather than bearing it on a sad note. When we undergo a trade of buying or selling, there are only 2 probabilities, i.e., either it will be in our favor or it will not. If it is in our favor, we are smart enough to handle our profits, but when it does *not* happen to be in our favor, that is the actual test of the trader. Thus, in my entire trading life, the Holy Grail I have known is to ***"Decide the Loss First before executing the Trade."***

There are many Traders and Investors who take advice from others and do the trades. I would recommend them that when anyone gives you advice for short-term or long-term investment, all you need to ask are 2 questions:

1. **The first question to yourself – How much risk I want to take in this trade?**
2. **The Second question to the one who has given you the recommendation – When to exit if you go wrong?**

If one receives answers to both the questions with 100% logic and not even 1% of emotional element involved in them, I believe he will not face any problem while trading. Subconsciously also, when your mind knows what is the extremely adverse condition, it relieves you of the stress, and you start thinking positive about the trade, leaving fear completely aside.

"When you think of only profits, profit never comes; when you think of losses, the loss never comes."

I will share my trade sheet with you, demonstrating the way I decide losses first and never the profits from trading/investing:

No.	Date	Name	Conviction	Risk	Buy/Sell price	Happy Loss	Quantity	Risk%	Inv_value
1	1.1.2016	XYZ	High	100000	100.00	95.00	20000	5%	2000000.00
2	1.1.2016	ABC	Medium	50000	100.00	90.00	5000	10%	500000.00
3	1.1.2016	LMN	Low	30000	100.00	85.00	2000	15%	200000.00

The picture given above is my trade sheet.

1st and 2nd column are for general information

3rd column: Name of the security

4th column: The conviction you hold for trading in the security

5th column: The risk level in quantitative terms that you would bear for the respective security

6th column: What price you are going to Buy or Sell? (I have given all buy examples here to keep it simple)

7th column: At what price will you exit the trade?

8th column: Let your risk level decide the quantity rather than influence the money management with the emotional elements such as greed or fear – Quantity of securities to be bought is in proportion to the pre- decided risk level.

9th column: Risk % on trade

10th column: Total Value or Exposure

Now, all depends on the Conviction – How much does one intends to lose? What is the risk of the trade? That is the Happy Loss – this must be decided before executing the trade. If this is done, it is assured that the individual is on the path of becoming a *212°: The Complete Trader*.

So, is Happy Loss only for Traders, not for Investors? No, Happy Loss is a must for both Investors and Traders.

"If we decide when to exit before we take the entry, and if we follow it rigorously, 90% of issues are cleared in Trading & Investing."

Summary & Learnings:

- Cutting Losses is the key to being a *212°: The Complete Trader*
- Stop Loss term should be perceived as a "Happy Loss"
- A loss which is booked to stop further loss is a "Happy Loss"
- Deciding exit Level before entering the Trade is the source of emotion-free Trading/Investing

3 Action Steps to be taken from this Chapter:

1. Action Steps:
_____

_____

Date to Achieve it: _____

Accountable Person: _____

2. Action Steps:
_____

_____

Date to Achieve it: _____

Accountable Person: _____

3. Action Steps:
_____

_____

Date to Achieve it: _____

Accountable Person: _____

Notes:
_____
_____
_____
_____
_____
_____
_____
_____

Chapter 5

Doing Things That Are DISLIKED

"In Trading, doing what you don't like will take you to the place you like."

In this era of motivational videos and convocational speeches, we hear **"Do What You LOVE."** It is, however, a myth. Everyone loves sitting on a couch, eating pizza with cola and watching TV. All of these provide only momentary pleasure. The fact is doing things that you don't like takes you on the route to success.

As no one likes to get up early, write a book, hit the gym, go for running, taking crucial decisions in business and other actions, which are not preferred by the majority, but they are the keys to success. This is how it goes in the arena of Trading/Investing.

Joel Osteen has stated it beautifully as **"flesh vs. spirit."** So what is the difference between flesh and Spirit?

Flesh: it is generally loud and we love to do it. It has short-lived benefits, but in long term, it is proved to be a bitter decision.

It refers to the things that we internally know are wrong, but we still proceed with doing them; we call it **"Instant Happy Syndrome."**

Spirit: Spirit is silent and works within our senses.

It might not make one happy instantly but in long run, it turns out fruitful and prosperous – we call it as a **"Delayed Happiness Syndrome."**

It is very hard to follow, but once it is adhered to, it makes an individual attain the Pinnacle.

Now how does this work in trading?

Flesh is what we love to do, and we call it as our **Instant Happy Syndrome:**

- To book profits earlier before any signal
- To avoid the Happy Loss
- To oversize positions
- To take instant gratification trades
- To listen to so-called "Market Gurus"
- To be undisciplined and to think in present, justifying it by stating that the future is uncertain

Whereas, Spirit Says:

- To be calm and to focus on strategy rather than thinking about markets
- To think for long-term and avoid short-term success and failures
- To take the trade in the best of the knowledge and systems, as far as they lie within our control, while the fluctuation in the market is beyond anyone's regulation
- We are not here to make a big chunk in short time; we are here to make consistent money in the long run

To excel in trading and investing, one needs to do the things which are tough and disliked by the majority, especially avoid what the flesh tells us to do.

I had a buy position in Aurobindo Pharma at 186 INR after nearly 17 "Happy Stops" – it was painful and not happy till the 18th trade came; it started inching up and went up to 250 INR, nearly all of my 17 stops losses were erased and I reached my breakeven point. My flesh started telling me that I should exit now as I have surpassed losses, as the price has reached the highest point, moreover, all the market gurus were suggesting profit booking in the trade. It was very hard not to listen to Flesh, as it is always louder and bolder, but I stopped watching the price of the stock and it inched higher and higher to a price of 500 INR. Everyone around me said, *"You don't have to be so Greedy, you should book it once set for all."* It was all flesh because my system-based trailing happy loss was not giving any signal to book it. After 8 months, it inched to 1100 INR and I exited as per system at around 1000 INR. It was the best derivative trade of my life (till date), only because I heard my spirit; I did the hard thing that proved to be a **"delayed happy syndrome."**

Remember that "95% of the Traders/ Investors will always listen to their flesh and the ones who listen to their spirit will always win."

I have researched and met nearly 100 excellent traders and investors and the most common commandment which they shared was **"One has to be disciplined."** Thus, **"To achieve what we like, we must do tasks that we dislike."**

Summary & Learnings:

- Doing the thing which one doesn't like in initial phase is the Key to being a *212°: The Complete Trader*
- Focus on what Spirit says and avoid what flesh is saying
- Choose Delayed Happy Syndrome over Instant Happy Syndrome
- To get the desired results, one must do what is disliked

3 Action Steps to be taken from this Chapter:

1. Action Steps:

_____

_____

Date to Achieve it: _____

Accountable Person: _____

2. Action Steps:

_____

_____

Date to Achieve it: _____

Accountable Person: _____

3. Action Steps:

_____

_____

Date to Achieve it: _____

Accountable Person: _____

Notes:

Chapter 6

The Don't Know Manifesto

"When I stopped Predicting I started Performing."

It is very easy to pass speculations on market; it's similar to playing with darts on a dart board, where someone hits the target or fails to hit it. The most significant thing is whether we want to make money or not? All we aspire is to be proved right. While being a research head in a broking company, proving my market prediction to be right used to give me immense happiness, but when I was right I had hardly capitalized, as I was in quest of proving my research right. Many times, I was right and I also went terribly wrong numerous times, but why, as a trader, we tend to predict the market, despite knowing the fact that **"PRICE IS GOD?"**

We need to understand who are we – Pundits, Tarot Card Readers, Astrologers – who want to be proved as Mr/Ms. Right – or Analyst? Or a Trader/Investor?

While attending social functions, the first question that is asked by the people who know that I am a trader is "What's next?" Be it a marriage or a demise. Initially, I used to give big detailed answers proving that I know everything, but eventually, I understood the fact that no one knows where the market is going to head, and everyone simply gives a random probability of future market predictions. No one

including the research reporters, the market wizards who come on TV – have the accounts of who has predicted what and what has been the success ratio. This is because there lies an extremely remote chance of predicting exactly what is going to be the actual future of the market, especially in short term.

Therefore, I have started following the **"Don't Know Manifesto,"** and anyone who asks me "What's Next in the Stock Market?" or any question that involves forecasting and prediction of the market, my fixed answer is **"I Don't Know (with a smile)."** To be honest, many times my flesh forces me to answer, but it's not worth answering the person asking such a question because:

- Is he is going to follow the predictions which I have told him? - Mostly NO
- Even If he does, am I aware of his risk appetite? What type of trades has he placed so far? Or what is his/her current financial status? - 100% NO
- If he follows my prediction religiously, and I was in long position while providing the advice, but if I turn bearish later, will I update him to go bear? - NO
- Do I have any benefit in predicting the future and giving free advice here and there, just to prove how knowledgeable I am? NO, not at all!

A Trader/Investor should also be very flexible in his views, just like a sports person, who has a very flexible body to handle in-nick-of-time conditions. If one gets stuck or becomes rigid in one direction, one position or one investment, it is very hard for him to survive in the market. While having the prediction syndrome, one gets subconsciously stuck in one direction and this is the reason he is not able to change the investment/positions as per the market trend. This might prove to be the biggest reason for making the highest losses and losing the biggest trade/investment of the lifetime!

When Crude Oil was at 3,200 INR (50$), one of the fellow traders who trades in crude oil futures, predicted that it won't go down from this level, moreover, being a technical Trader, he also had all the fundamental reasons favouring his prediction about why Crude Oil won't go down. Eventually, Crude oil prices started hitting south, but because of his predictions, he could not initiate the fresh sell trade in Crude at 48$. Therefore, from thereon, crude oil prices started sliding down till 1,800 INR (22$) and he missed the single biggest trade of his career. At Turtle Wealth, we religiously follow the **"Don't Know Manifesto."** We initiated that crude oil trade and it proved to be one of the best trades for us.

Therefore, from today onwards, if anyone asks you **"What you think? Where is the market heading?"** single answer with sheer humanity should be **"I don't know."** Why shall we predict an answer? Rather we should focus on the Systems, the Markets, and the Price will eventually lead us to be *212°: The Complete Trader*.

Summary & Learnings:

- Price is God, rest all are conversations
- Stop predicting, start performing
- Be a Professional Trader/Investor, don't try to be an analyst
- Making money is more important than being right in the eyes of the public

3 Action Steps to be taken from this Chapter:

1. Action Steps:

_____

_____

Date to Achieve it: _____

Accountable Person: _____

2. Action Steps:

_____

_____

Date to Achieve it: _____

Accountable Person: _____

3. Action Steps:

_____

_____

Date to Achieve it: _____

Accountable Person: _____

Notes:

_____
_____
_____
_____
_____
_____
_____

Chapter 7

The Biggest Myth and the Biggest Boon

The biggest myth which is popularly sold in this market is **"Buy - Hold & Forget,"** i.e., the best way to make money in stocks – it is partially right also – but the mass applies it on the stocks which are underperforming as well. The biggest fear I face is when I talk to investors during Bull Period, and they claim **"I am not going to sell the stock forever."**

Now, let's talk about numbers, in Indian Stock Exchange BSE, there are around 5000 stocks which are listed and, out of them, if I take the best probability, only 2% of the stocks will be consistent wealth creating stocks in future, i.e., 100 stocks. Thus, 98% is the probability that we might not get the wealth-creating stocks. Out of those 2% stocks, there is 98% probability that even if one has bought the stock at the right time, he might not hold it until the end and will rather exit due to sheer greed of achieving higher profits, or in a fear of fall in the current prices. Now the probability is 0.04% of buying wealth creating stocks and holding them until their best time like HDFC, HDFC BANK, KOTAK, INFY, PIDILITE, ASIAN PAINTS, Colgate, Apple, Nike, Berkshire Hathaway, Google etc. This is applicable to every market and in every country.

There Are 3 Biggest Myths That Prevail in the Markets:

1. Making money in Stock Market is very easy
2. The Stock market is for Short-Term Money Making
3. Only Buy position can make Money

So many people come up with their free advice, saying if you had bought X, Y, Z stock, you would have made huge money. I completely agree, but through my experience, there were numerous incidences, when stocks sounded extremely lucrative to me at one point in time, while at the later stage, they held no whereabouts. What about those incidences?

In the market, we never discuss the mistakes committed by others, but I would like to state the fact that I don't watch Stock market channels at all. A few days ago, I was having a day off, and I just thought of checking markets, which, however, turned out to be my biggest mistake, as I turned on the TV to watch the Stock market channels, wherein, they were highlighting their previous prediction that had turned to be right. The schedule given to the speakers/analysts in such channels is of nearly 10 hours daily, wherein nearly 10 analysts speak, out of such huge data, certainly there is a minimum of 2% chance that their predictions get in the right place – my 6-year-old daughter can also do it. Thus, by ignoring the remaining 98% times when they go terribly wrong, they are bestowed as the accurate market forecasters and we go gaga about them.

We as the audience are displayed with the examples of Mr. Warren Buffett, Mr. Peter Lynch,

Mr. Benjamin Graham, Mr. Rakesh Jhunjhunwala etc. I agree that they might have made a stunner through the concept of **Buy & Hold,** but they have also booked losses and exited from the stocks which they had bought for "Long Term" as they failed to perform, so the idea is that *"Ride the Winners, Exit the Losers,"* whether it is for the Long, Medium or Short term.

Many broking houses run a wealth study, talking about the past wealth creating stocks; it is like doing the research on already performed stocks and now such researches are undertaken in masses. However, such exercise holds a very less probability of attaining the results at the same level.

So why is it that every book, every analyst, every fundamentalist, every mutual fund investor majorly focuses on only BUY & HOLD syndrome? Whereas, the biggest Boon of the Market is one can even SELL and HOLD. None of the businesses give an opportunity to an individual to make money in the bear market and, as per the prediction, there is 98% probability that the stock will be a wealth destructor rather than a creator.

Why should **"Short position"** be taken in only companies which are high in prices? We have a Turtle Trader who had taken a short position in numerous shares that quoted in a single digit; his formula was simple that it is all about percentage; when everybody thinks there is nothing to lose – as the stock has already gone down to single digits – it means it has much more to lose.

I truly believe in it, and I practice it as well – a Trader/Investor should have an active short portfolio as well as long Portfolio, many hedge fund companies do such practice actively, and they have attained high popularity because of it.

"In the Bull market, everyone can make money, but the one who makes money in Bear Market also is a true 212°: The complete Trader."

Summary & Learnings:

- There lies 0.04% probability that one will have a Multi-bagger Stock
- Taking Short position & Hold is Equally Important as Buy position & Hold
- "I am not going to sell this stock forever" is the riskiest statement

3 Action Steps to be taken from this Chapter:

1. Action Steps:

_____

_____

Date to Achieve it: _____

Accountable Person: _____

2. Action Steps:

_____

_____

Date to Achieve it: _____

Accountable Person: _____

3. Action Steps:

_____

_____

Date to Achieve it: _____

Accountable Person: _____

Notes:

_____

_____

_____

_____

_____

_____

_____

_____

Chapter 8

3 Types of Traders & A Master Formula to Be the Wealthiest Trader/Investor

"The 2 most difficult things in the stock market are to accept a loss and not to realize a small profit." – Andre Kostolany

In the past decade of trading and investing, I have gathered one significant insight and it is above all the others which I call as the **Thumb Rule or a Holy Grail.**

There are the 3 types of traders in this world, be it in trading of equity, derivative, currency, options or agri commodities; this rule applies to everything. It also applies to Sports, Business, Casino and every sphere of life. If one decides to go through it, I can claim it with surety that there is a high probability to create substantial wealth over a period of time.

1st Type of Trader: Unlimited Loss - Limited Profits (Big Loss - Small Wins)

This is the kind of trader who generally falls for instant gratification trades; he is majorly an amateur who seeks short-term profits; he has a target but no happy loss or risk management.

Let's understand this trader in depth. Here, he wants a small chunk of money leveraging big money or trading in high quantity, without realizing that if he goes wrong what might be the loss.

Mr. A buys a stock at 100 INR and decides that he would book it at certain price or profit at 105 INR, 5% is great, but if you ask that at what price he will exit, he has no answer to it. There are more than 80% such traders. Eventually, if this trade does not work, it gets shifted to a form of investment with a popular saying, *"I feel this company is good for long term, why to book loss in it?"*

It is exciting and thrilling, isn't it? The trader wants to portray that he/she is smarter than the market, wants to earn a quick buck and party hard.

Believe me, such type of a trader is going to blow up soon once there is a 10–20% fall in markets, all previous trades profits will be flushed. The Irony is that majorly everyone starts with this stage, and the one who goes ahead understands that this is a suicidal/fatal way.

Never try it; if you are practicing it, STOP IT!

2nd Type of Trader - Limited Loss - Limited Profits (Small Loss - Small Wins)

This is the kind of trader who is somewhat better and educated than the previous ones, but he always seeks an opportunity and always repents on missing one or not capitalizing on the opportunity – he is a predictor as well as an analyser.

Let us take an Example- Mr. A. buys a Stock at 100 INR and fixes his stop loss at suppose 97 INR and targets at 105 INR or 107 INR. Such trader is like a technical analyst, finding support and resistance, Head & Shoulder, Doji, Morning Star and all the Jargons you can come up with. They always have a target for everything, and seek advice to fix the target. The Question that pops into my head is **"What is that Target?"** These targets are set by following most of the technical analysts that one watches on TV. We say that this is generally **"Treadmill Trading."** You enjoy trading; you get excited too, but at end of the day, you are where you were before.

I am not criticizing such kind of trading, but I would state that it will not make you millionaire or billionaire; at the end of the year, your broker will be richer than you by such a type of trading approach.

I have tried to make hundreds of different trading systems for the second type of approach, which gave profits initially, but at the end, they turned out to be wastage of time and money.

3rd Type of Trade: Limited Loss – Unlimited Profits (Small Loss – Big Wins)

"You have to lose a lot of battles to win a War." – Sun Tzu, Art of War

However, this is boring, hard and unbearable, but the truth is, this is the only way to be able to perform exceptionally in Trading/Investing.

"Boring is Exciting in Trading/Investing."

Let us take an example: Mr. A bought a stock at 100 INR, knowing his downside, let us take at 95 INR, but he holds no idea of where to book the profits, he simply keeps trailing his stop losses at every level. This example is relevant for both sides, i.e., long and short.

Name any great businessman, any great trader or investor, he would belong to the third category of trading only. Here, I am talking about serious transactions of money.

Everyone would recommend you to be the first or second type of trader, but a real *212°: The Complete Trader* is the 3rd category trader where the **"Risk is Defined, Profit is INFINITE."**

Whenever I take a trade, or someone comes with an Investment idea, my first checklist is to find which category the system falls in. If it falls in the first or the second category, the level of attractiveness is ZERO.

Believe me, I have saved millions by not investing in the first and second categories and have made much more by falling in the third category.

Even giving money on interest basis or on loan, would fall into the category of the first type of investment.

The most common question from the traders or Investors who approach for mentorship is, **"Despite having Knowledge, experience, why are we not able to excel in trading or investing?"**

I ask them which type of traders were they? Mostly the answer turns out as first or second, so why does this third type of a trader makes the most of it.

Type of Traders	Win Ratio	Loss Ratio
1st & 2nd Type (Amateur Trader)	80% (Small Wins)	(Big Losses) 20%
3rd Type (212° Trader)	20% (Big Wins)	(Small Losses) 80%

The Market is a Zero-Sum game with many losses and few wins, so if there are 3 types of traders and we try to figure out who wins and who loses the most, we would find that the first and second types of traders possess a higher accuracy to win as their payoffs are very small, while when they do losses, they are very huge. Thus, when this third type of trader has drawdowns, then the amateur or retail mentality traders would be having a great time, but once the third type of trader gains a huge chunk, the amateur category must be going through the toughest time, and there is a possibility that they might end up wiping off whatever they had earned from numerous small trades.

Let me demonstrate this with a simple example of how the 3 types of Traders would be trading:

Trader	1st & 2nd Type of Trader	3rd Type of Trader
1st Trade	+10 Points	−10 Points
2nd Trade	+20 Points	−20 Points
3rd Trade	+20 Points	−20 Points
4th Trade	+15 Points	−15 Points

5th Trade	+10 Points (Increased the Quantity in Over confidence as every trade is giving Profits)	–10 Points (Increased the Quantity in confidence as every trade is giving losses so a big Trend is about to come)
6th Trade	–200 Points	+200 Points
7th Trade	+20 Points	–20 Points
8th Trade	–400 Points	+400 Points
9th Trade	+30 Points	–30 Points
10th Trade	–90 Points	+90 Points
TOTAL	–565 Points	+565 Points

(This is a tested trade example of 2 types of Traders in NIFTY Future Index)

With the Trade sheet, what we observed was:

- % Win doesn't matter; it is all about how much we make when we are right, and how less we lose when we are wrong
- 1st and 2nd types of Traders had a great beginning, and in overconfidence, they increased their positions too – we tend to do the same, don't we? In 10th Trade, they lost nearly 565 Points – without taking the added quantity into the consideration – despite getting 70% of their trades right.
- 3rd Type of Trader was only right in 3 Trades, but he won with 565 Points – without taking the added quantity into the consideration.

- It is very hard to control yourself when everyone is earning and you are losing, it is, however, the part of life of a *212°: The Complete Trader*, as they say-

"Lion gets to hunt a few times; deer gets to eat more frequently, but it's the lion who gets to eat deer all the time."

Summary & Learnings:

- "Unlimited Profits and Limited Losses" is the Billionaire's Way
- Boring is Exciting in Stock Markets
- If one has 20% win ratio, he still has the scope for making more
- Be a Lion in Markets, not a deer

3 Action Steps to be taken from this Chapter:

1. Action Steps:

_____

_____

Date to Achieve it: _____

Accountable Person: _____

2. Action Steps:

_____

_____

Date to Achieve it: _____

Accountable Person: _____

3. Action Steps:

_____

_____

Date to Achieve it: _____

Accountable Person: _____

Notes:

_____

_____

_____

_____

_____

_____

_____

_____

Chapter 9

The 4 Monkeys Approach

The greatest of the great Mr. Mohandas Karamchand Gandhi or our beloved Gandhiji introduced us to the 3 monkeys approach, which was impressive, and I tried to execute it thoroughly in my personal life as well as trading. Thereafter, I came up with the 4 monkeys approach, where the 4th monkey belongs to the current generation. For a 212° Trader, this four-monkey approach is closely correlated with Trading/Investing.

1st Monkey: Not to Hear Anything Bad

In Trading/Investing, there are 2 voices we hear – first is from the external world and second is from the internal world within us – both the voices should be heard in a selective manner.

The voice of external world is inclusive of news on mobile, market gurus on TV that keep roaring about the future predictions, YouTube videos, brokers, and friends that keep loading us with unlimited information. Gaining knowledge through these sources is useful, but trading/investing based on their recommendations can prove to be risky.

Many years ago, I had selected and decided to listen to only a few individuals who had done exceptionally well in their life as a Trader/Investor, whose ethics and Integrity levels were incredible; rest were just conversations for me. However, if tomorrow, Mr. Warren Buffett buys stock named XYZ Ltd. and says that he is very bullish for next couple of decades, I would never run and buy that company as Mr. Warren Buffett and Mr. Rohan Mehta are 2 different individuals.

Similarly, if some so-called Market Guru claims that market is going to collapse, I won't unwind my positions just because he has said so; I would just close my ears and focus on my strategy, system and money management.

The external forces are still easy to handle; the hardest part is the internal voice which blows hot and cold to exit from the positions with small profits, not to take losses, not to adhere to the systems; to choose the easier path to satisfy the flesh. The inner voice is the blend of both the conscious and subconscious minds, considering the past experiences of trading, but *212°: The complete Trader* must limit himself and try to understand what is being told by the flesh and what is being suggested by the spirit.

One can also try to say lots of affirmations to control the inner Flesh. If I name my affirmations, I chant more than 100 times a day what Mr. Charlie Munger has said, **"We don't have to be smarter than others; we have to be more disciplined than others."**

Thus, Stop:

- Listening to Radio or TV for tips and market predictions
- Listening to people who are not successful in trading and investing
- Listening to your flesh, which is the easiest thing to do, but simultaneously most dangerous as well

2nd Monkey: Not to Watch Anything Bad

There are so many things that we watch every day which affect our decisions on trading and investing and, in the end, we might have made just mediocre results.

The biggest stopover suggested here is watching daily prices and getting stuck to the screens.

In one of the interviews, Mr. Bill Dunn, one of the world's renowned Trader and fund manager at Dunn Capital Management, shared that very few people at Dunn capital are stuck to the screens. From that period of time, I stopped watching live markets; I asked myself, 'Why do I need to watch the market updates every day, every hour, every minute?'

My systems are in place; my happy loss is placed well in advance, then why to keep a record of every tick, every move that gives an impulsive behavior in trading and investing and proves to be the biggest curse as a Trader/Investor?

If a builder wants to build a building, he will select a land, he will go to a civil engineer and an architect, and finalize the design for the building – he will put a lot of effort to finalize the structure. Once he finalizes it, then he will go to a civil contractor with a plan to build the building, and there, he would finish his responsibility. Does the builder watch the building getting constructed brick by brick? No, he will just review it periodically; now same is the case with trading – a trader (builder) decides what he wants to trade, makes a system or strategy (architecture) and gives it to a dealer (Contractor). Is there any need for him to watch every movement in the market tick by tick (brick by brick)? If only reviewed periodically, I assure you that the profits (building) would be much better and, at the same time, you would receive plenty of free time that could be given to your health, reading, family, society etc.

Our Mind is easily convinced and gets excited when we watch crime, porn or negative interview which gives us "Instant Excitement." Stop watching them. Knowingly or unknowingly, they influence your mind, and thus, our Trading/Investing also gets affected.

3rd Monkey: Not Saying Anything Bad

I have taken numerous training on "Self-Talk," through which I learnt that it has been scientifically proven that 90% of the diseases take place with what we say.

In the Holy Bible, it is written: **"The power of life and death is on the tip of our tongue."** Moreover, it is very rightly said that we don't need any enemy; our tongue alone does it all for us.

My Daughter's favourite phrase is *"Dad, be aware! Whatever you say, is what happens."*

When I meet traders or investors, and I ask, "How's it going?" The most common answer is "Not Good," i.e., the market is not good, trends are not coming etc. As it is said, "What you say is what happens." It's so important to mind our words; we don't get to know but subconsciously they come into being, it's better to chant some affirmations that keep giving us positive energy.

Some of my affirmations:

1. Rome was not built in a day, but Rome can be destroyed in a day
2. I don't have to be smarter than others; I have to be more disciplined than others

3. My work is to trade with the systems; the God will take care of the rest
4. My Patience will be tested, but my conviction will be rewarded
5. I am here to be a Billionaire!
6. Never say Never
7. What is the maximum loss I can bear?
8. Trading is a Business, not a Casino!
9. Profit is only Profit when it is taken out from the account; rest are just a numbers
10. This Too Shall Pass

Make a list of your affirmations and stick it somewhere in your trading room, so that you can watch the list on a regular basis. Record them in your voice and keep playing them as the background music; play it in your car, you will not even notice and your subconscious mind will register it forever.

These affirmations make me more focused and more grounded in my self-talk.

When anyone asks me about my trading, my straight answer is, *"Its going Amazing; I am getting more focused and disciplined day by day."* I also add, *"I am the luckiest person to possess trading as my Business."* Do I answer like this for the sake of the person asking this question? No, it's for me and my subconscious mind.

4th Monkey: Not to Think Bad

The first 3 monkeys are familiar to all; here is the admission of a new kind of monkey on the list.

I have always thought myself to be the **"The World's Best Trader & Investor."**

When we are not speaking, listening or watching, what do we do? "We think and we think even more." These thoughts play a key role in the structuring our personality and the way we are. As Lord Buddha has rightly said: **"You are what you think."**

In Trading as well, it is very important to think in a structured manner; I don't encourage only to think of earning billions and millions; it is all about being realistic, as *Trading is all about NOW!*

So, when I make a system or place a trade, my thoughts are always centered on:

- How much Time can I afford to lose?
- How much money can I afford to lose?

When we think of the worst at the beginning itself, it replaces all the negative emotions from our mind, and once the trade or system starts getting executed, all we think about is:

- Am I 100% disciplined?
- How can I improve upon making better systems?
- What are the major threats associated with my systems?
- For bringing regular improvements in the trade or the systems, I do the KIDS analysis of my trading behavior and understand the areas of improvement and where I need to stop

These four-monkey approaches will hand-hold an individual to become a *212°: The Complete Trader.*

Summary & Learnings:
- Stop Listening to the people who have not earned money in markets
- Stop Watching price tick by tick
- Tame your tongue; let your Profits do the talking
- Whatever you think, you will become

3 Action Steps to be taken from this Chapter:

1. Action Steps:

_____

_____

Date to Achieve it: _____

Accountable Person: _____

2. Action Steps:

_____

_____

Date to Achieve it: _____

Accountable Person: _____

3. Action Steps:

_____

_____

Date to Achieve it: _____

Accountable Person: _____

Notes:

Chapter 10

The 3 Most Essential Hobbies of a Trader/Investor

I follow the podcast of Mr. Brett Steenbarger "Chat with Traders" – I would also recommend you to hear it regularly – Here, Mr. Steenbarger stated that for being the best trader, one must have a hobby other than trading, and I was completely convinced with such thought process.

These days I have been hearing to Mr. Atul Suri – one of the most-followed traders in India – I witnessed him talking more about scuba diving rather than trading.

For being *212°: The Complete Trader*, it is very important to have 3 major hobbies other than trading. I meet a lot of traders who claim to be extremely passionate about markets and follow charts and track markets nearly 18 hours a day. Such practice can prove to be fatal for traders. Sometimes, you need to leave your trades to destiny; all that is required is to have a happy Loss and stop tracking – believe me, great trades are the ones which are left alone. So, as per my research, *212°: The Complete Trader* philosophy, to pass the time apart from trading in a day, one should have at least 3 essential hobbies for sure.

1st Hobby: Reading

212°: The Complete Trader should be an extensive reader, but the topic should not be restricted only to the markets, it could also be:

- Spiritual
- Productivity
- Biography
- Psychology

"Socrates read a book even on his last day to die more intelligent."

These books can make us a better person, and eventually, an excellent Trader/Investor. When I met Mr. Warren Buffett and Mr. Charlie Munger, Mr. Munger told me about the number of hours Mr. Buffett reads, and it is beyond anyone's imagination! As he reads for more than 11 hours a day – I still cannot imagine how can anyone read for 11 hours a day? Here, the first thought that comes to our mind is, 'He is so Rich, he can read for 11 hours a day, but we can't afford to.'

Right? And my question here is:

"He reads because he is rich or He is rich because he reads?"

2nd Hobby: Sports

Sports is more or less the same as trading – both demand for investing a lot of time in developing mastery; both need practice, pain, and persistence. One faces victories, gets defeated numerous times in both the circumstances and keeps growing with the passage of time. In my life, I follow 2 kinds of sports, i.e., running and cricket.

Our inner self keeps asking us to quit at a premature stage; this also happens while running, as our inner self keeps pestering the mind to quit, considering the pain in the legs and the shortness of breath, but once we stop following and listening to it, we become a better person in 2 aspects:

- Great Health
- Increased Stamina of never giving up

To be honest, I don't like running every morning, but I have made a habit of running anyhow. This year, my target is to run a full marathon, just to ensure the above-stated 2 stamina to remain at an all-time high.

Cricket exists in every Indian's blood; it is, of course, the love for the game that makes us follow it, but it also teaches us many things that are related to trading:

- Bowling and Batting are 2 important actions in cricket; similarly, in trading, Long and Short are the significant actions/positions
- It all functions with a teamwork in cricket; in trading, it is all about the team of the strategies you execute
- Cricket necessitates patience, especially during the test matches – the longest time horizon game; played for nearly 5 days – similar is the case with trading and investing
- Cricket has 3 major formats – T20, One Day and Test Matches, with the corresponding formats of short term, positional and long-term in the case of trading. All the formats account for different strategies in both cricket as well as trading
- Sportsmanship is more important than winning the game; same discipline is ensured in case of trading

3rd Hobby: Learn Music

I was totally inspired when I met Ed Seykota and he played the **"Whipsaw Song"** in IFTA at SFO – 2013. Music, again, is an art form that takes a lot of time to learn and gain proficiency, and thus, it demands a high degree of persistence, practice and lots of patience. Music holds a significant influence on an individual by soothing his mood and making him more focused. Moreover, it releases the day-to-day pressure of ups and downs in the market.

Through the cultivation of the above-stated 3 hobbies, one comes close to being a *212°: The Complete Trader.*

Summary & Learnings:
- A 212°: The Complete Trader should have other hobbies to ensure a balance
- Reading, Sports and Music are some of the best Hobbies that one can develop
- Cricket is much like Investing and Trading with 3 different formats of the game

3 Action Steps to be taken from this Chapter:

1. Action Steps:
_____

_____

Date to Achieve it: _____

Accountable Person: _____

2. Action Steps:
_____

_____

Date to Achieve it: _____

Accountable Person: _____

3. Action Steps:

_____

_____

Date to Achieve it: _____

Accountable Person: _____

Notes:

_____
_____
_____
_____
_____
_____
_____
_____

Chapter 11

The 6 Key Reasons Why 90% of Traders/Investors Face Losses

We have surveyed and met nearly 10,072 account holders, where an individual or a company has either traded or Invested over last 10 years, and here's what we have found:

95% of the accounts were in losses, rather huge Losses; this analysis is, however, a decent one; the actual results are even worst. There is one significant finding from this survey

the basic reason behind such losses include 6 common mistakes that were found across the Investors and Traders. I believe that if we avoid committing them, we are already ahead of masses. I am sure these are the mistake committed by all major traders and investors across the world.

1st Mistake: Tendency to Book Early Profits & Late Losses:

This can be considered as the biggest and major mistake of all times, wherein, if one books even the small profits, he gets so excited that he starts cutting out positions ASAP – as soon as Possible – to cash in the profits. He feels that it's a proud moment, as he has made quick bucks, while in reality, believe me, this is the biggest mistake as a Trader/Investor. Similarly, if he gets a loss, he would tend to hold it with an expectation that the same will pull up the prices again.

Let me explain this with an example: An individual has bought a share of XYZ Company at 100 INR after seeing all the fundamentals or technical aspects of the company, thinking that he would be a long-term investor in the company, if tomorrow, the stock opens at 105 INR– if he is lucky – everything around will pressurize him to book the profits and cash in the money, such as:

- His Own Instant Gratification Mind: He might plan to imbibe the additional 5 rupees that he had earned
- His Broker: With an intention to earn brokerage out of his transaction of buying and selling of securities
- His Friend/Colleague/Spouse: They might say, "Take the Profit. Who has seen tomorrow? It is uncertain"

It is totally fine if one closes his account and banks all the profits with an intention of never returning, but if he is going to trade again, trust me, such a habit will never let him earn big.

Likewise, if one buys a share of XYZ Company at 100 INR and the stock open at 95 INR tomorrow, his approach gets reversed, as he will think of holding with a perception that "I am a long-term Investor" and will not sell it. Here's when everyone will support him in his decision such as:

- His Own Instant Gratification Mind: I will not take a loss for sure; I am an Investor and stock must have reacted because of some selling pressure
- His Broker: the broker will suggest to hold and rather advice you to buy more at the reduced prices
- His Friend/Colleague/Spouse: "Never take a loss, you forgot Warren Buffett's rule?" – However, Warren Buffett has himself exited many Investments in

major losses, recently in TESCO – ref. Berkshire Hathaway Annual letters

Let me ask a Question: Imagine that a Businessman is holding 10 diverse businesses. After a quarterly review, it was found that 5 businesses have done substantially great 2 have reached their break-even point and remaining 3 have encountered losses. Now as a Businessman if he has to terminate some businesses, which of the following will they be?

a. The Performers

b. The Break-evens

c. The Under Performer/Loss makers

I am sure a normal human being with the basic IQ of 100 will answer C, now I ask the same question from the perspective of your portfolio of trading and investing, does it go in the same way?

In the above survey, everyone would opt for the option C, however their trading approach was found to be completely opposite.

How to overcome this?

As one of the best traders, Mr. Ed Seykota quoted, **"Ride your Runners, exit your Losers;"** this is the first rule of being a *212°: The Complete Trader.*

2nd Mistake: Averaging a Loser

The biggest SIN of all time in Trading is **"Averaging a Loser;"** nothing is a bigger mistake than this, we believe that major losses which are especially committed in investment is because of addition to the losing positions, one of the veteran investor of India, Mr. Rakesh Jhunjhunwala says,

"As a rule in the market, I will never ever average."

In the initial stage, one will find this mistake as one of the commonly-committed mistakes; moreover, it happens frequently with amateurs; it has happened to me as well. While committing such a mistake for the first time, its not very troublesome, if it becomes a habit, it holds the power of blowing up the entire investment.

It is a general mentality of being hesitant in booking losses, if the stock is going down and one is holding a long position and if the stock goes up and one is holding a short position. In both the cases, averaging the losses gives relaxation to the mind on the verge of hope.

While buying, averaging can cost the maximum of the invested amount, as the extreme it can go to is zero, but while having a short position, it can cause an infinite amount of loss and can even make an individual go bankrupt.

We, at Turtle Wealth, had taken an oath that irrespective of anything, we will neither invest nor trade in the investment with constantly falling prices.

3rd Buying Low & Selling High:

"Buy Expensive where one fears to Sell, Sell Cheap where one feels Greedy to Buy."

It's all about Price! Majorly, all basic investment books suggest that an individual is needed to buy at cheap prices and hold it for long, but general mass has misunderstood the concept. It is believed that a stock which had gone up is expensive, and the one which had gone down is cheap.

However, the stock or commodity which has gone up or down has a reason behind it. For a trader, it is all about playing with price and if price heads North, there must be something good about the company. I will illustrate it with an Example:

I don't like buying Airline Stocks, but I had seen a very good breakout in the stock and I bought Jet Airways at nearly 52 Week high and it increased further thereafter. All the fundamental reasons such as fall in the Crude prices at 5 years low etc. led to first profitable quarter for the company after 7 non-profitable quarters. Similarly, a real estate stock was quoted at 11 INR and there was a negative breakout on the stock and I took a short position in the stock and exited at nearly 8 INR (Trend Reversal), i.e., 40%. Subsequently, reasons like huge debt, negative rating etc. led to further decline in the share prices, thus, this decision proved to be a profit maker, however, apparently, it was a loss-incurring deal.

High makes High; Low makes a New Low!

If one buys stocks which are trading at their **"FRESH"** new all-time high and short stocks which are near their all-time low, one will make much more profit than doing vice verse. While taking a period of 10 Years for backtesting in any country, one will be able to understand that buying high & selling low is the virtue and trade secret of all *212°: The Complete Traders*.

4th Mistake: Not Investing in Knowledge First

"Lesser is the Knowledge, more is the Tuition Fees."

It takes nearly 14 years for a person to complete his schooling. Thereafter, to be a doctor, one needs 6 more years, 3–4 years for completing the bachelor's degree, further, it would require 2 to 3 years for post graduate courses, then only one is able to work and earn. Thus, it means that after losing 1/4th of the total lifespan, one becomes eligible for earning, but as a Trader, one wants to earn from the very first day he starts trading. But without any formal Knowledge or Mentor, there are only remote chances to succeed.

It has also been realized that we spend so much money on food, clothes, luxuries, child education, but when it comes to attaining financial knowledge, we tend to avoid it. In my seminar, when I asked someone from the audience for the reason behind not bringing his teenaged son along, for attaining some financial wisdom, he responded by saying that the son hardly needs it. While growing in schools, we learn by attaining the basic education and cultural education given by our parents, but when it comes to financial knowledge, it is found to be nil in the majority, even in the top executives of firms, whom I have mentored over the years.

Mr. Robin Sharma always states that: ***"Learn more to Earn More."***

One can gain knowledge from reading great books of Traders/Investors, taking training through successful traders, establishing an association with the knowledgeable Traders/ Investors and following up with a mentor.

The simple math is- the reward for the amount one invests in knowledge is 10 times

5th Mistake: 95% Are Biased to Do Only Long; 5% Are Biased to Do Only Short

I have addressed numerous traders, investors, brokers, associates, top executives, investment bankers and the first and foremost question I ask them is:

"What is the beauty of our business – trading business – that no other business on the earth has?"

Almost 99.9% are never able to answer it correctly. Also, I would like the readers of the book to try answering it, as I believe one needs to adore the game of trading to an extent that, even in his subconscious mind, he finds no business to be better than trading/Investing.

The Answer is: *"This is the only business on the earth where Money can be made even by taking a SHORT POSITION."* For instance, if I find the Property market going down, can I Short it? No. But, if I find a stock getting weaker and weaker, can I short it? Yes and that's legal.

I have been interacting these days with a lot of MBA Finance Students who are learning the art of Trading and Investing, but they are never taught to short in the market. Additionally, the other day, I was watching a documentary on traders of Chicago, wherein it was stated that the activity of keeping any company short is considered as a sin; in the real-time arena, if one fails to short, the survival in the market for a longer period becomes difficult.

In any basic investment book, one would find only BUY and no SHORT, however, the actual magic and beauty of business lies only in going short. As it is a commonly known phenomenon, gravity functions faster than anti-gravity. Contrariwise, Mr. Raamdeo Agrawal (the co-founder of

Motilal Oswal) once stated that while doing a short, if one fails to be vigilant, he can turn bankrupt at a faster pace and it is actually true!

While taking a probable case in Indian Stock Markets, in National Stock Exchange, there are 2629 Scripts Traded as on 09/03/2015[1]. Let us suppose, over the period of 5 to 10 years, only 5 to 7% great companies will be able to compound the wealth by more than 18% to 25% YOY, while remaining companies will prove to be the distrusters of wealth. Taking the example of the Bubble of Harshad Mehta, wherein a lot of stocks did a crazy rally. Out of them, nearly 10% of stocks are good performers even in today's date. Additionally, taking the example of Dot Com Bubble, due to which many companies do not hold any existence today and are rather only on papers, while some are still functional and performing great, like Infy, Wipro, HCL Tech etc. This means on a count of 1 to 10, there is an 80% probability that one particular stock will not perform well, and it makes a lot of sense to short such stocks.

Now the question arises as to how will we be able to know whether the stock is going to perform in future or not, the answer is "PRICE" – the price will suggest everything.

For an Investor, it would be fine not to short the stocks or Index, but for a trader, if he stays only Bull, I will be worried that he might get slaughtered.

6th Mistake: Paying Less Commission

"In Stock Markets, Costly is Cheap & Cheap is Costly."

This will probably be something that one would have never heard of – in a survey, the most shocking and common mistake found in masses was paying less commission to the broker – now one would wonder how could this be a mistake? Here's how it is: When trading or investing first came into practice, no one looked at the cost, rather more emphasis was laid on the right principles and way of trading. In the initial years of Indian Capital Markets, the brokerage commission was as high as 10% per trade, as the investors or traders never thought of doing lots of trades and made a consistent earning. Coming to the present conditions, where the commission is as low as zero because the frequency of trading has increased, it is ruled by instant gratification trade and that is the time one digs a grave for himself.

The brokers who are comparatively costlier in terms of commission, but focus on risk management and not breaking the compliances are the ones whom should be selected over the ones who provide easier and cheaper options. Thus, I advise you to get a broker who is not aiming at increasing the number of trades or the volume of shares, rather, is strict in terms of money management, provides the right wisdom and pokes the clients if he finds them going in a wrong direction.

One is advised not to do these 6 Mistakes in the beginning of being *212°: The Complete Trader*.

Summary & Learnings:
- Riding the profits, Exiting the Losers
- First Invest in Knowledge and then in Markets
- Don't get into the trap of the low commission brokers; it's better to deal with the ones who charge high commission

3 Action Steps to be taken from this Chapter:

1. Action Steps:

_____

_____

Date to Achieve it: _____

Accountable Person: _____

2. Action Steps:

_____

_____

Date to Achieve it: _____

Accountable Person: _____

3. Action Steps:

_____

_____

Date to Achieve it: _____

Accountable Person: _____

Notes:

_____

_____

_____

_____

_____

_____

_____

Chapter 12

The 7 Most Important Questions to Ask before Taking a Trade

Why is more important than HOW?

Before taking any positions in markets, it is a must to find your "why?" Once we find the answer to why and sort it, losing or winning does not matter much. Moreover, if we find the answers to 7 significant questions before having taken a position, irrespective of long or short and investing or trading, the clear picture of "why" is found and addressed. Thus, the trade can be considered as completely planned and structured. This is an inspiration from the book named *Trend Following* by Michael Covel.

1. What to Buy or Sell:

This is the most significant question to be asked in a trading system – what one is going to trade or invest in, among the equities, options, commodities, currency and Agri Commodities.

Generally, one should trade in the following:

Highly Liquid – Index, Commodities, ATM (At The Money) Options

Highly Cyclical – Sectors like Real estate, Banks, Oil, Metals, etc.

One should invest in stocks which are defensive and more on consumption themes.

It all depends on what market one trades in and what his risk appetite is. My trades are in:

Commodities – Crude Oil, Lead and Silver Equities – 7 Different cyclical sectors such as capital goods, banks, infrastructure, real estate, diversified, finance and pharma

Index – NIFTY, Bank Nifty Options – At the Money Options.

For Instance, generally, I am more focussed on trading in index and commodities, so I prefer trading in NIFTY, BANKNIFTY, SILVER, LEAD, and CRUDE, as they are backtested and their volatility matches my personality.

2. When to Buy or Sell:

Once it has been decided what to buy, the second question is – when to buy? 'What' would be set as the technical or fundamental indicators, based on which the buying and selling decisions will be generated.

For example:

1. All-time fresh high, that is done after at least 10 years – the longer the years, the better is the breakout, while keeping the Happy Loss as the previous month's low
2. Closing above or below 50 days Exponential Moving Average
3. Closing above or below 200 days Simple Moving Average

Please note: Do the proper back testing before executing the system, considering your risk appetite.

These are very simple type of trading strategies, to begin with, and I assure you, these systems hold the potential of delivering returns beyond one's expectations; they have the power to give much more consistent returns than one usually expects to attain.

3. When to Exit:

There are no Guarantees in this business, but "The only thing that is guaranteed is that there will be losing trades."

As one holds an entry plan, planning the exit point is equally important; we trade with a desire that we will not go wrong anywhere, but this is the major myth; we have all the right to go wrong, and we surely will.

The exit is a decision that is undertaken when the trade of either long or short did not go as per the expectations, and thus, one desires to take the opposite position.

Let me explain it in a simple manner: All of us buy Insurance policies – Health Insurance, Life Insurance, Office Insurance and Home Insurances. Why? Do we want to Die or get sick? NO, but we take the probability of any misfortune happening in future and thus, insurance can prove to be a savior. A *212°: The Complete Trader* always considers stop loss as an insurance for the trading so as to save the destruction of the capital in case of any unexpected market volatility. Thus, the incurred loss, even after exiting at the stop loss, can be considered as the "Premium," i.e., paid to attain an insurance policy. Through such mindset, trust me, one will not face issues associated with losses.

4. When to Book Profits?

This is a question which totally depends on the system to system or trader to trader.

212°: *The Complete Trader* doesn't book profits until the time the trend changes, irrespective of a short-term, positional or a long-term trend.

Profit booking is for Amateurs; riding Profits is for Professionals.

As Mr. Jessie Livermore quoted, *"Profit Takes care of itself; Losses never do."*

There are 2 Animals in Jungle – a Sheep and a Lion. Sheep eat every day and is able to gather food easily, whereas, A Lion waits for the prey and takes 5–10 sheep together and feasts only ones or twice a week. Now, it's the same in the markets; Sheep is the trader who books profits here and there, whereas Lions are the traders who earn the profit equivalent to 5–10 Sheep- like traders and once in many months.

212° Traders are indeed LIONS.

5. How much to Buy/Sell?

This is a very crucial question as the sustainability of the traders lies in this question. Different type of risk takers and their leverage systems are:

Defensive Traders: Those who don't like more ups and downs in markets and are happy with decent returns should not take leverage at all. For instance, if someone is trading 1000 NIFTY with a price of 8000 INR, he or she should have 80,00,000 INR as an investment and trade, i.e., total

Contract size or 0 leverage, as per the rules of SEBI with PMS, no leverage.

Moderate Traders: One is open for **"Calculated Risk"** that can go for 1, 2 or 3 times leverage if someone is trading NIFTY 1000 with a price of INR 8000, he is required to have INR 40,00,000 or 30,00,000, i.e., 30% to 50% of total Contract size; this means that taking calculated risk surely depends on the calculation of your system's drawdowns as well.

Risky Trader: One should not trade in this category, being a *212°: The Complete Trader*, but here are some areas such as commodities or currency, where the overall age of the asset is not that wide, so considerably, one can take leverage accordingly.

However, doing this with equities is not recommended, and in the remaining cases, 1:5 is the maximum leverage that is recommended to any trader.

"I believe there are 2 things which can kill a trader: 1. Leverage 2. Lack of Patience."

6. When to Scale up:

Generally, this question depends on the designed trading/Investing system; the first 5 questions can be known through books or other sources, but this question is unfamiliar to masses and should be given huge emphasis in order to excel in trading, i.e.,

When to add up? When does a system hit a drawdown of 15%? There are chances of systems giving the best reversal, or maybe, when the stocks clear a specific level, that is the point when one should add up to a stock or commodity.

Similar to how we generally add up when Draw Down (DD) is at its nervous level, whenever one starts feeling that there is no ray of hope, that is the time when a new trend is coming.

When to Pyramid the profits, system to pile up the positions? This subject is taken in the *"Magical Money Management"* Chapter.

7. When to STOP:

Since we have decided that we will give any system 999 days to perform, if it fails to perform the way it had been back tested, we will review whether the system is the problem or the market has reacted in an adverse manner. Only through reviewing, we will be able to make out whether to continue or terminate the trade.

Like how we were Trading in Nickel. For the previous 3 years, it was dragging the portfolio down. In the third year, we decided to exit from it, and in today's date, we realize it to be a wise decision.

This is the Card I follow before taking any positions. If all the questions in this card below are not answered, it's very risky to take a Trade/Invest.

6 Questions	Questions	Answer
1	What to Buy/Sell	
2	When to Buy/Sell	
3	When to Exit in Loss	
4	When to Book Profits	
5	How Much to Buy/Sell	
6	When to Pyramid	
7	When to Stop	

It is a rule to answer these questions and then only take the trade. If one starts adhering to these 7 Questions, it's akin to having the one Extra Degree to be a *212°: The Complete Trader*.

Summary & Learnings:

- To answer the 7 Questions before doing an Investment or a Trade
- Filling the card will be boring and tough, but after filling it, one will reach the zone of Serenity
- This is the best way to be an emotionally free Trader/Investor

3 Action Steps to be taken from this Chapter:

1. Action Steps:

_____

_____

Date to Achieve it: _____

Accountable Person: _____

2. Action Steps:

_____

_____

Date to Achieve it: _____

Accountable Person: _____

3. Action Steps:

_____

_____

Date to Achieve it: _____

Accountable Person: _____

Notes:

_____

_____

_____

_____

_____

_____

_____

_____

Chapter 13

The Bull, Bear and Pig Phases

"Bull Makes Money, Bear Makes Money, Pigs gets Slaughtered – Wall Street – II"

The Market is generally considered to have 3 phases: Bull, Bear, and Pig. When the market is trending up, it is known as the bull phase, while if the market is going down, it is known as the bear phase, and when the market is not showing any movement, it is called the pig phase – derived by Turtle Wealth. However, it is very tough to judge the current phase of a stock, index or commodity solely through data rather than going by popular market hypothesis; let's understand all the 3 phases in depth.

Bull Phase:

"Bull" is derived from the historically known fact that when a bull attacks, it lowers its head and uses its horns to thrust the opponent up in the air. Hence, a bull market trends upwards while previously being low, and thereafter it rapidly climbs up; also the horns of the bull are always upwards.

The question is: How to derive that it is the bull phase? This is a theory we have derived from a decade-long research; moving average has been one of the key indicators to derive a justification, irrespective of whether it was price wise or the Balance sheet wise. These days, Moving Average is available for free from any website or mobile application, as after many combinations, we have derived logical reasoning involved behind when an Index, Stock, Commodity or Currency is in Bull Phase: Medium-term to Long-Term Time Frame or Horizon.

These are the 2 condition to be in Bull Markets:

1. When 75 EMA (Exponential Moving Average) and 200 (Daily Moving Average) are Positive below the close price
2. When 75 EMA Value is higher than 200 DMA

For Instance, on 21.2.2017, if NIFTY 75 EMA is 8488 and 200 DMA is 8413 and close price is 8907:

1. 75 and 200 both are Positive
2. 75 EMA value is higher than 200 DMA

"The bigger is the gap between 75 EMA and 200 DMA, the Stronger is the Bull Phase."

This indicates that Index is in a "Bull Phase," At the same time if one assesses the fundamentals, something positive would be happening in index/stock, one will find positive rating on stocks provided by research & institutions.

Bear Phase:

"Bear Market" is derived from the ancient times. When a bear attacks, it swipes its gigantic paws down, bearing down on its opponent with full force. Therefore, it makes sense that a bear market is one that plummets. Also, historically, the middlemen involved in the sale of bearskins would sell skins they were yet to receive. As such, they would speculate the future purchase price of these skins from the trappers, hoping that the prices would drop. The trappers would earn profit from the spread – the difference between the cost price and the selling price. These middlemen were eventually known as "bears," short for bearskin jobbers, and the term stuck for describing a downturn in the market. Conversely, because bears and bulls were widely considered to be opposite to each other due to the once-popular blood sport of bull-and-bear fights, the term bull stands as the opposite to bears.

Another theory about the juxtaposition of bears and bulls comes from the Elizabethan era of blood sports "bear baiting" and "bull baiting." Arenas filled with people would watch either a bull or bear, chained in the middle of the ring, and then be attacked by a pack of dogs. Such practice had begun as early as the late 1500s and was prevalent in England until 1835. Considering that the terms bull and bear markets originated in around 1714, many people believe that this is where the idea of bulls are the opposite of bears was derived.

The question is: How to derive if it is Bear Phase? This is a theory derived by us after research of a decade, Moving Average has been one of the key indicators to come to a justification; it can be based on Price wise or the Balance sheet wise. After many combinations, we have derived logical reasoning involved behind when an Index, Stock, Commodity or Currency is in Bear Phase: Medium-term to Long-Term Time Frame or Horizon.

These are the 2 conditions of being in bear phase:

1. When 75 EMA (Exponential Moving Average) and 200 (Daily Moving Average) are Negative (below the closing price)
2. When 75 EMA Value is lesser than 200 DMA

For Instance, let's take the example of the day before Lehman Filed Bankruptcy on 15th September 2008 – as taking the data of 12th September 2008; 13th and 14th was a weekend – Dow Jones 75 EMA was 11675 and 200 DMA was 12295 and the end of the day close was 11421:

1. 75 and 200 both were Negative
2. 75 EMA value is lower than 200 DMA

This indicates that the Index was in a "Bear Phase," At the same time if one assesses the fundamentals, something negative would be happening in index/stock, one will find a negative rating on stock provided by research & institutions. A day after the Lehman Crisis was derived and the world collapsed, Dow Jones went to as lower as 7882 in a single stretch; this was Indicated much before the announcement of such a news in the markets. This concept will be applicable to any stock, currency or commodity across the globe and even on those who begin trading and investing on the other planets. If we compare with the fundamentals as well, there would be certain issues in the stocks; the profits would be getting lower due to some discrepancies and the stock rating would also be on SELL SIDE.

Pig Phase:

This phase has been invented at Turtle Wealth inspired from the famous dialogue of Wall Street II. This is a phase where nothing happens, irrespective of whether one buys or sells, he loses money, and thus, it is the dirtiest time for an Investor or a Trader which is probably the reason why it is called a Pig Phase. This is the time when 90% of the mass exit the markets, one starts taking the shortcuts to earn money, and

212°: The Complete Trader takes a break to learn more and more; this phase is generally called as **"Trend Less Times."**

The question is: How to conclude that it is a Pig Phase? Moving Average has been one of the key indicators to determine this phase as well, whether it is Price based or the Balance sheet based. Post the assessment of numerous combinations, we have derived logical reasoning involved behind when an Index, Stock, Commodity or Currency is in Pig Phase: Medium-term to Long-Term Time Frame or Horizon.

Here is the one condition to be in Pig Phase.

1. When 75 EMA (Exponential Moving Average) is Positive/Negative and 200 (Daily Moving Average) is Positive/Negative from the day's closing price, either one of them – 75 or 200 remains positive or negative in comparison to closing price, and also the stock is in range and no major breakout is found.

For Instance, let's take the example of ACC (Stock in NSE – India) 75 EMA 1418, 200 DMA 1508, Close Price 1438.

1. 75 EMA is lower than Closing Price and 200 DMA is higher than the Closing Price

This indicates that the Index was in a "Pig Phase;" it is better not to fight with the stock till it enters the bear or bull phase because if one fights with the Pig, he himself will get dirty while the pig will enjoy the fight. It's a good time for option writers to make some decent money. This phase, if compared with Fundamentals, will show that the stock is not doing anything great – no major earning upgrade, no major innovation; also the stock is least tracked by masses.

One of the most appropriate examples of "Pig Phase" is Reliance Industries – one of the biggest companies in India; it has been a Wealth Creator as well. However, from 2009, it entered Pig Phase, and just a day later, when they launched some innovation in Telecommunication Industry called "Jio," it entered the Bull Phase. If one would have understood the theory very well, one would have saved a couple of years, opportunity cost and lots of money too.

Safe Harbor: I am not suggesting to buy, sell or hold an Index, Stock, Commodity or Currency. This is just for the Educational Purpose to derive the knowledge of a Trend Direction.

212°: The Complete Trader uses this research as one of the most scientific, unbiased indicator to know about the phases; with the above wisdom, forget about earning the money; millions will be saved by not taking wrong steps and getting trapped, as it has been rightly quoted:

"It's better to be vaguely right than precisely wrong."

Chapter 14

The 2 Best Tools for Trade & Investment

"Trading/Investing has to be Sophisticatedly Simple."

In my 10+ Years' Experience of being a Professional Trader & Investor, I have understood not to make Trading & Investing complicated, and to make it as simple as possible.

"More the Complexity, more the hopelessness."

I started my career as a Fundamental Analyst and one of my Mentor Figures Mr. Bharat Sadrani, who made a software program on Technical Analyst, encouraged me to use it. It was in 2008 when no Fundamentals were working, so I tried my hand in technical method and I found it to be one of the simplest ways to judge a stock or Index. Thus, I owe my success to Mr. Bharat Sadrani whom we generally denote as "Kaka (UNCLE)."

Having spent many years of being a Technical/System expert, I have come across a lot of Traders on Facebook/Twitter/Email asking the most common question, "Which tool should I use in Trading?" – What Indicator, what Software, etc., and to their surprise, I never use an online Tick-by- Tick software. I always use an EOD Software – "Bazaar Indicators" and "Spider" – that cost me a total amount of 20,000 INR p.a., renewable on yearly basis. People get shocked by listening to this, because they expect some 10–15 screens and numerous online software programs at work, as this is the way it is depicted in the movies or documentaries. Thus, the next question is, "What are the tools that are Implemented?"

Well, I use the 2 simplest tools in Technical method and they are:

1. Moving Averages
2. Swing

Most important Tools for Investing are:

i. Profit After Tax

ii. Growth

These tools could be considered too simple to be implemented for undergoing big trade/ investments, as we live in the illusion that – *bigger the trader/Investor, higher is the complication of the tools implemented by him*, but the reality is its inverse.

All the systems that I have made are formed through such indicators only, and I can claim it with surety that one will find them magical. I would like to admit that I have never learned an in-depth technical analysis, and I am still not aware of technical jargons such as Head & Shoulders Pattern, Doji, etc. I have learned only these 2 indicators in depth, and only they have helped me to thrive as a Trader/Investor for all these years. These are not applicable only to Trading; they also hold equal relevance in investing as well, like a Stock closing below 200 Daily Moving Average is called Negative. In a similar manner, if you plot the P.A.T., Sales Chart of the company and draw Moving Averages, it will also indicate the trend of the company.

Owing to my experience, I would like to encourage the readers to get a good hold on any 2 relevant indicators in either Technical or Fundamentals to judge their decisions. As they say in an Old Axiom, **"Too many cooks Spoil the Soup,"** similar is the case in Investing/Trading – Too many Indicators result in a completely confused and under-confident state.

Summary & Learnings:

- Complex is Hopeless
- Find your 2 Indicators that will dictate your Trading/Investing

3 Action Steps to be taken from this Chapter:

1. Action Steps:

_____

_____

Date to Achieve it: _____

Accountable Person: _____

2. Action Steps:

_____

_____

Date to Achieve it: _____

Accountable Person: _____

3. Action Steps:

_____

_____

Date to Achieve it: _____

Accountable Person: _____

Notes:

_____

_____

_____

_____

_____

_____

_____

_____

Chapter 15

212° Investment Thesis

Being a Full-Time Trader and Investor, I have made several systems on trading, but have made fewer and specific thesis on Investment. This is the basic reason behind my preference to buy or sell any specific stock more on a long-term basis. Such theory is framed with the collective wisdom attained from all the veteran investors across the globe and the experience derived by implementing them in my real life.

There are generally different types of Investors like Value, Contrarian, Micro, and Macro. I am focused more on Growth Investing. My thesis states that there should be a very simple mode of investing; I believe investing is the simplest form of making money, however, holding on to the stocks for a longer duration is very tough.

Although such Investment Theory is not a Holy Grail, but it's the profound way to Invest in some Great Stocks.

1. Growth is Important Indicator:

Over the period, many fundamental analysts have assessed the best tool for investing among P.E., E.P.S., Intrinsic Value, etc., but for me, the growth of the company is the biggest indicator – envisaging how much a company can grow with the market – is the key to any big Stock Picker. If one can estimate growth and the opportunity, all other data are of no use. Annual Profit after Tax is the data which I prioritize during the fundamental review.

2. Products:

The Product is the key to the Business Growth. If the product is a brand, and there is a craze in people to possess it, it is a company that should not be missed for investing.

How can one know about it?

Check Social Media, when People post about the product, and they are happy and feel proud to have it– it is the company you are seeking for investment, for example:

1. Eicher Motors: When many proud owners post about buying a Royal Enfield and going to Ladakh etc.
2. Apple iPhones: Nothing much is needed to say about it; still Apple is a status symbol for many
3. Maruti: When they buy Maruti Suzuki Cars, and they feel special and secure about it

(**Note:** These are just a few examples and not the stock recommendations to buy.)

This is one of the ways to know what is happening, and the product speaks for itself; also the product should be a must-use product – even if there is a recession, the product should still be used like P&G or Pidilite etc. Here, the product is sold in the name of the brand and the company also enjoys a high- profit margin.

One of my best investments was in Welspun India that makes the towels for Wimbledon Championship and it has a superior quality product, within a span of 2 years, the stock went 9 times its original price.

One should be in love with the product. For example, you have Maruti in your portfolio and but you drive some other car, this is a big mismatch. It's similar to how Mr. Rakesh Jhunjhunwala always wears a Titan Watch on his wrist, Mr. Warren Buffett always sips coke, and I always eat a Britannia Biscuits.

3. 4 Pillars that will suggest a company's future:

1. **Employee and Dealer Relationship:** The 1st Client is Employee and the 2nd is Dealer. Generally, before investing in a company, I would ask the company's employees certain basic questions such as:

    i. How is the attitude of management towards you?

    ii. Do you get Salary on Time?

    iii. How's the culture in the company?

    iv. Would you invest your salary in your company's shares? Etc.

From this, I come to know about the company's worth – the 1st rule is that if the company is not paying salary on time to their employees, however well the company may be, I would never invest.

Secondly, I would go to the dealers of the company and ask about their products, services and the payout they get. I have a friend who has a Lingerie store in Surat, so I asked him about "Loveable Lingerie" as a company. He told that he was not that satisfied, so I asked about PAGE Industries (Jockey) and his answer was, "We have to shut our shop if we stop selling it." Hence, it was simple for me to judge.

How would anyone know about it? LinkedIn is the best website to find the employees and interact with them. For the dealers, find one, go as a customer and get all the details out – yes, if you end up buying the product, it means that the investment can be done.

2. **Creditors:** Every company has a tie-up with banks for payment and transactions. Many companies take loans, cash credit, overdraft facilities, etc. The level of Integrity of paying the dues and interest demonstrated by the company says enough about the management and their way of doing the business. If the bank has an exceptional credit score for the company, it is an additional advantage for the company to be sound and structured.

3. **Customers:** The most important part is, "How much is the customer satisfied with the product and services of the company?"

If you ask me, I am the most-satisfied customer of HDFC Bank, I will never choose a bank other than HDFC Bank, or maybe iPhone as an example, go and ask the customer of a company about their experience with the company, they will give you an insight. For instance, ask a Royal Enfield owner about the Bike, they are the "For-Free Sales Manager" of Eicher Motors; they just love it, or maybe Harley Davidson – they have chapters around the city for the H.D. riders. This is not only for the listed companies; this is also applicable to invest in the Unlisted Companies, where you find that the people are crazy about the product and they will even stand in a queue just to buy that product. Another example would be the case of Nokia to Blackberry to iPhone. In all 3 cases, the customers loved them but as any shocking news or bad publicity comes into the picture, the clientele gets shifted, thus, we need to assess the customer preference and shift our investment accordingly.

4. **Management Lifestyle:** *"Both the Promoters and Investors of a company cannot live a flamboyant lifestyle simultaneously"* In many companies, I have seen promoters who lived a Flamboyant lifestyle – spending lavishly, having a yacht, huge property, Private jets. In that case, the investor will never earn much in the same way, if the promoter lives a simple life, there is a very high probability that Investors will be rich.

There are Millions of examples where this has happened:

a. Some big Billionaires move to Billion-Dollar worth houses, but investors might not have earned any wealth

b. A Promoter who gives expensive mobile phones as return gift in a personal party; his company's stock prices went 80% down from the listing price

c. A Promoter buys an expensive yacht for his wife; investors have lost tremendously in all his companies

d. A Promoter who has so many villas, cricket team, and other extravagant expenses; the company has closed down

e. A Promoter who cooked up books of accounts for living a luxurious lifestyle; his company crashed and now he is in jail

In the same manner, there are promoters who have just done work with integrity in their whole life and given back to the society, and simultaneously their companies have also done remarkably well are as follows:

a. Mr. Narayan Murthy – Infosys

b. Mr. Azim Premji – Wipro

c. Mr. Warren Buffett – Berkshire Hathway

d. Mr. Deepak Parekh of HDFC & HDFC Bank

e. Tata Group, and so on

Also, I see how honest they are with their respective spouse, **"If they cannot be honest with their spouse, how can they be honest with their shareholders?"**

You can know the company's Promoter's lifestyle in today date easily through Twitter, social media, etc.

With these 4 pillars, one can envisage the strength of a company and its vision for a long term.

4. Market Leader:

It's always great to invest in the companies that have a good market share in their area. When we invested in Maruti, it was enjoying a market share of 49%, and today, it still has a market share of 45%. In the 2nd highest economy, a market share of 45% is extraordinary. Similar is the case with P&G's 3 products – Vicks, Whisper and Huggies that enjoy a great market share in their respective area. I like the company who is a leader in the market and enjoys the position.

5. Investing in the Inflow Stage:

There are probably 3 stages in a company's life:

    a. Value Inflow: Where the company has just started to grow. The company can grow exponentially high, and the growth trajectory is much larger – **Time to Enter**.

    b. Value Stagnation: Where the company has shifted from value inflow to value stagnation. Here, the competitors of product and services enter the market; thus, because of competition the market share declines. Also, the valuation is getting higher; here the P.A.T. should be reviewed if the Profit Increases YOY, still there can be some scope for improvement – **Time to Book Profits, or review more**.

C. Value Outflow: Here, the value shifts from one area to other. It can be Cameras to Mobile, Computers to Laptop, Simple phones to Smartphones, etc. Here, I would exit the stock and start finding again some Value inflow company – **Time to Exit**.

6. Numbers:

After the above 5 steps, the number comes into consideration, I give very less importance to numbers while investing as there is a high probability that the balance sheet is cooked, but the above 5 points cannot be manipulated. Still, I have certain calculations that I do:

a. The last year's PAT should be at its highest in the past 5 years

b. It should be technically above its 200 DMA Daily/ Weekly & Monthly all

c. If it has more reserves, then the market cap with 0 debt, it's the icing on the cake

d. Debt to equity is generally not a big concern to me, but still, I review the adequate utilization of the debt.

7. Writing thesis:

After all these stages are passed, the most important and last stage to answer are the following questions: Investment Checklist

   a. What do I love about the company and why will I invest in that company? (Maximum 500 Words)
   b. Have I checked above stated 6 Steps? What is my thesis for the same?
   c. When and how will I pyramid my positions?
   d. If given an opportunity, will I be a real partner of the company?
   e. Do I have a conviction of even selling my home to buy this company?
   f. When will I exit the Investment? (Minimum 5 Points)

Make a report on it, and stick to a board, so whenever you have any temptation to book the profits, or not to exit when anything wrong happens, you may review it. One of my checklists is that if the management does anything which breaks the Integrity, I will sell the stocks immediately, and I did the same when Welspun India was found guilty of breaking Integrity with their dealers in the USA.

Summary & Learnings:
- Creation of own Investing System is very important
- Invest in Products You Love and Use
- Boring businesses generally deliver better returns
- Invest at the Value inflow stage

3 Action Steps to be taken from this Chapter:

1. Action Steps:

_____

_____

Date to Achieve it: _____

Accountable Person: _____

2. Action Steps:

_____

_____

Date to Achieve it: _____

Accountable Person: _____

3. Action Steps:

_____

_____

Date to Achieve it: _____

Accountable Person: _____

Notes:

_____

_____

_____

_____

_____

_____

_____

_____

Chapter 16

Formula No. 21

"A prudent person foresees danger and takes precautions."

Proverbs 22:3

I have been fortunate enough to have a brain of both an Investor and a Trader, which is very rare to find, but one must have it as he grows as a Trader/Investor. I have always been known for my stock-picking techniques throughout my career. I was blessed enough to pick some of the best wealth creators; however, I have also possessed some stocks which held the capacity of wealth destruction – but I was prudent enough to exit with HAPPY LOSS.

This is probably the only formula which talks about when to **"Exit in a Stock."**

In the past 2 years, I discovered that trailing Profits Stop with a systematic strategy is very important in Positional or Long-Term Investment. Tactfully, you don't know at the time of Investing which stock is going to be a Multi-Bagger; Market Gurus call that "Buy and Hold," where history proves that most of the stocks which go northside dropped down to southside very fast as well. While Investing, manytimes, I have bought a good stock at the right time, but I could not find the strategy to exit in profits; I tried taking 100% of my Investments out when the stock inches up to 100%, but that too was not the right way of investment.

In the Journey, I found the "Formula no. 21" – If one buys a Stock at 100 rupees, there are 2 probabilities, stock may go up or go down. If it goes down, we *212°: The Complete Traders* always have a Happy Loss, so we don't worry; we don't have an upside Target as we believe in "Big Profits and Small Losses." So, if the stock goes 110–120–140–150+, at a certain point, it will correct or react; now we have 2 fears within us:

1. We don't want to exit just because it has gone up; we want to sit tight till the stock is bullish
2. If stock comes down again, we don't want to miss out the gains we already have on the table

In this case, "Formula no 21" works amazingly well. Let us understand this with an example.

Mr. A has bought a stock at 100 rupees. Let us assume that it starts the upward journey until it is not above 21% of the price he bought, this rule is not applicable, until that time "Happy Loss" is the Exit Point, so till the Price of 121 – The rule of 21% does not work.

Above 121, whatever level the stock goes, from the highest price, when it breaches below 21% and closes below that price, it is the time to exit in the stock. Let us assume the stock which he bought at 100 goes till 191 – stop loss is equal to 150 – so his Exit Point will shift up to 150. If the stock closes below 150, he will exit the stock.

Why one needs to exit the stock? There are 3 Probabilities which happen with a stock:

1. The Stock price goes up
2. The Stock price goes down
3. The Stock price remains in a range. By applying the Formula no. 21, the 2 odds are at our side. If the stock

goes down, we don't have a problem. If the stock is in the same range, we are in benefit, and with these 2 odds, we have 2 major benefits:

a. We can invest the money in new opportunities
b. We can remain in cash and book substantial profit without any emotional thought process.

So when to re-enter the stock? Yes, we should re-enter the stock again if it shows strength. Let us understand again with the same example.

When the Stock which we exited at 150 with a high of 191, again when it closes above 191 on Daily Charts, we will again re-enter with the same theory of 21% again.

One would think that it would be a loss-making deal, yes, it would be, but a NOTIONAL Loss. We don't have any financial loss into it, but yes, we are buying the same stock again at 21% more costly value. If we see probability wise, from 10 Stocks, if there comes an exit in 8 stocks with this formula, out of those 8 stocks, 6 would go down or consolidate at the same price and in the remaining 2 stocks we need to re-enter with higher cost, it is still more beneficial, but if market tanks out from there, one would be all in cash.

Like in 2008, through the application of this theory, one would have been 100% in cash by January end and millions would have been saved.

If the stock is really very strong Fundamental Wise or Price wise, it has a very remote chance that stock will break its 21% downside. Most of the time, it will reverse from that area, like Dabur, HDFC Bank, Asian Paints, Pidilite, etc. have rarely broken their 21% zone.

If you are not a very aggressive decision maker, you can apply this same formula on Weekly or Monthly Charts as well.

With this Formula, in Bull phase, one may lose some percentage of profit, but in a Bear market, one would be in cash, as the stocks that remain in the portfolio, are the winners.

Safe Harbor: Before executing this Formula, back test it on your personal decision of Investments from last 10 Years. If you get great results, I am sure you will, then go ahead.

"My Best Holding Period is neither Long Term nor Short Term, but it is until the time I make Profit from it" -Rohan Mehta

Summary & Learnings:
- Formula No. 21 is knowing when to Exit in the Stock
- Holding on to non-performers is also a Loss
- One must be swift in re-entering the stock as exited, without emotions

3 Action Steps to be taken from this Chapter:

1. Action Steps:
_____

_____

Date to Achieve it: _____

Accountable Person: _____

2. Action Steps:
_____

_____

Date to Achieve it: _____

Accountable Person: _____

3. Action Steps:

_____

_____

Date to Achieve it: _____

Accountable Person: _____

Notes:

_____

_____

_____

_____

_____

_____

_____

_____

Chapter 17

Magical Money Management

Of all the Chapters, Money Management is the chapter that possesses the soul of a Trader/Investor and for this book, it's the most boring subject; the least talked about topic, but if it is not managed well, it will come like a thief one night and steal everything one holds.

Money Management is all about taking the right amount of risk, according to one's nature and personality. Let us say we drive a car on the highway. There are generally 3 lanes: one is the attacking lane, one is the moderate lane – where generally trucks run – and one is the defensive lane, so when you drive the car, which lane would you prefer?

If one drives more on attacking lane, he is more of an aggressive investor/Trader who wants to take a calculated risk and doesn't want to miss any opportunity. If one drives on the moderate lane, he is more of a whole brain thinker, who would like to take a balanced approach. If one drives on a defensive lane, it's more obvious that one thinks to be safe and sound. Let me put this in a table for better understanding:

Lane	Risk Profile	Leverage	Trades/Invest In
Attacking	High – Aggressive (Calculated Risk Taker)	Calculated Leverage as per the opportunity	Stocks, Commodities, Midcaps, Small Caps

Middle		Moderate	0 Leverage, will trade/ Invest in what is available	Index, Commodities, Large Cap, Midcaps
Side-Line		Defensive	Always on Cash – Nimble-footed to take Risk	Bonds, Fixed Deposit,

This generally is the best way to identify one's personality and do Money Management accordingly, the 212°: *The Complete Trader* is one who knows how to shift gear in all the 3 Lanes, as per the availability of opportunities in the market. Many times, I am very aggressive, to totally sideline to moderate. I also shift my gears as per market opportunity and the trend.

An Investor disease is called Rhinophobia where one cannot control the temptation of buying or selling the stocks as one has got the cash; it's just like a habit of smoking or drinking that one cannot control; this is the biggest suicidal disease for an investor. The Magical Money Management is to be banged harder when there lies an opportunity in a system/investment with Cash, Courage, and Conviction. There is no standard rule for the exact level of Money Management; 2 things should be always taken care while doing the Money Management:

1. One should get good Sleep, after taking a position
2. If one goes wrong, he should not go broke

In my Trading/Investing career, I have come across 2 best Money Management Techniques which I call "Magical

Money Management" Techniques. These 2 Techniques will amplify the probability of you to attain that 1 extra Degree that will make a difference as a Trader/Investor.

1. Pyramiding in Profits:

"As Averaging in losses is a SIN, averaging in profits is a Virtue." I understood this formula very late, but I strongly believe that this is the only way one can excel as a Billionaire. This is the toughest part of the game. 99% people cannot hold Profits, and in this scenario, I am advising to add more, why? Initially, post taking a position, either for Trading or investing, no one knows whether it would be favorable or adverse, it's better to take a lesser position in the initial phase. Once the position – either it is long or short – starts becoming favorable, add up at each breakout level. If anyone follows the technicals, on the Investment side, add up as the company does growth on the profit side. Now, the biggest question is "When to exit?" On the Trading side, one can use **"Formula No. 21,"** or can sell as per the system's "Happy Loss"; on the Investment side, sell as per the thesis.

Of all the things, one thing is for sure – your highest position should be in the Trade or Investment which has the highest returns.

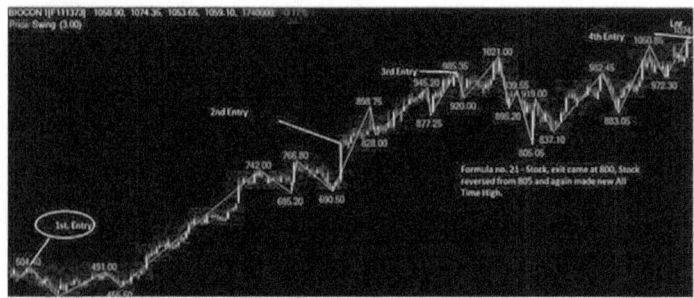

We bought Biocon Ltd. at 500. We again re-entered post a new breakout at 800, again new breakout came at 985, again at 1074. My average stop loss was at 800 according to "Formula no. 21" but it reversed. Today, my highest exposure is in Biocon as it has performed well; the same we did in Maruti as well. When we bought Maruti, initially, its Profit after Tax was 1600 Cr., then next year it became 2392 Cr., as more the Profit came, more positions we had in Maruti on Investment side, as one has to get it clear on which Thesis he/she is buying/selling a company. One also has to be clear on when to pyramid it – with logical reasoning, the conviction goes stronger and stronger.

99.99% Mass can't do this; it is the toughest part of being a Trader & Investor to pyramid the profits, not only when the stock is 10–20–50% plus, but also when the stock is 200–300% Plus, **"If you can pyramid, you have achieved the top level of being a 212°: *The Complete Trader.*"**

2. Martingale Money Management:

A martingale is betting strategy that was originated and widespread in the 18th century in France. The simplest of these strategies was designed for a game in which the gambler wins his stake if the result of a tossed coin comes out as heads, and loses it if it comes out as tails. The strategy states that the gambler is supposed to double his bet after every loss so that the first win would recover all previous losses, plus win a profit equal to the original stake. The martingale strategy has been applied to roulette as well, as the probability of hitting either red or black is close to 50%. This is one of the lessons which has changed me completely as a Trader. This Money Management is generally for such System Trader/Trend

Follower who specifically works on **"Bigger Profits and Smaller Losses"** or **"Unlimited Profits and Limited Losses."**

Trend Following is like a spring; the more is the spring pressed, the bigger will be it's bounce. If we apply the Martingale Theory in Trend Following, I can claim it with surety that to do losses over a period of time is very tough.

How Does It Work?

One must add up positions in +1 format post every loss position. If the position is exited with no Profit and Loss, still one has to add up, so more are the losing trades, more are the positions. As Trend Following says, more the drawdowns, higher is the probability of a Bigger Trade, as when the big trade will come, one will be having highest positions. After that bigger trade, one must again come to the basic positions. Let us understand this with a live backtesting example of Martingale.

No.	Buy	Sell	Points	Martingale	Martingale P&L	Cummulative P&l	Simple P&l
1	27000	27000	0	1	0	0	0
2	27000	26000	-1000	2	-200000	-200000	-100000
3	25000	26000	1000	3	300000	100000	100000
4	25000	26000	1000	1	100000	200000	100000
5	27000	26000	-1000	1	-100000	100000	-100000
6	27000	26000	-1000	2	-200000	-100000	-100000
7	27000	26000	-1000	3	-300000	-400000	-100000
8	27000	26000	-1000	4	-400000	-800000	-100000
9	26000	26000	0	5	0	-800000	0
10	26000	29000	3000	6	1800000	1000000	300000
11	29000	29000	0	1	0	1000000	0
Total			0		1000000		0

This is a general back testing on Gold – Indian Price. The lot size is of 1 kg = 100 points. It is a Long–Short System, with Stop and Reverse as Strategy; it has Number, Buying Price, Shorting Price, Points Earned/Lost, Martingale is no. of Contract, Martingale Profit or Loss, Cumulative of P&L of every Trade, Simple P&L if one would have done on the same number of contract size, i.e., 1 Contract.

In 1st trade, we traded one contract – we exited in no profit no loss; as 2nd trade, we traded 2, we got a loss; as the 3rd attempt, we traded 3, we got a profit; so, in the 4th trade, we came back to 1 again; in 5th trade, we did the base quantity as in 4th trade, we did profits; in 6th trade, we did 2 contracts as the 5th trade was a loss; in the 7th trade, we traded 3 as the 6th trade was a loss; in the 10th trade, we traded 6 contracts as all previous 5 trades were in loss. In 10th trade, the spring was pressed very hard due to previous whipsaws, and we got the big trade of 3000 points, i.e., 10,000, cumulative P&L came out positive as the 11th trade was again with base quantity.

It's very easy to understand; now the total is very interesting. The total points earned is 0 but we made a profit of 10,00,000 rupees. If we would have done with the equal quantity in each trade, we won't have earned any money, this is the power of Martingale.

If one's systems are with a high frequency of trades, then one can set an upper limit of contracts to be traded, like I had decided that I will trade maximum 1500 BANK NIFTY, with a base quantity of 400. In this Money Management system, one has to set the base quantity and upside quantity; one should also have **"Cash, Courage and Conviction"** to trade this. There will be instances when we would fear from trading further, but I assure you that **"One Trade will change your Life."**

My 10 Learnings of Money Management:

1. Always keep 6 Months of contingency fund of one's monthly expenses in Banks or Liquid Fixed Deposit; never invest or Trade from that money

2. Have Enough Life, Health, Office and Home Insurances for Calamities
3. Never buy a Liability on the profits earned from Trading
4. Never increase or decrease positions just because last trade/Month/Year went profitable
5. Focus on the Black swan, ask yourself, **"If something goes wrong, where will I Die?"**
6. Always Diversify in different asset classes tactfully; I Trade in Stocks, Index, Commodities & Invest in Midcap and Small Cap
7. Never Count your profits before they are booked, and do not brag about it
8. Profits are only realised when they reach the bank accounts statement; in your Trading account, it is just an additional capital
9. It's okay if Money Sleeps for some time
10. Never lend money to someone for helping them and if you do, do not expect them to return it back

Summary & Learnings:

- Most of the time of a Trader/Investor should be spent on reviewing and planning of Money Management
- Pyramiding is a Virtue
- Martingale is the key to a Trend Follower's Money Management
- A single Trend has the power of changing our life

3 Action Steps to be taken from this Chapter:

1. Action Steps:

_____

_____

Date to Achieve it: _____

Accountable Person: _____

2. Action Steps:

_____

_____

Date to Achieve it: _____

Accountable Person: _____

3. Action Steps:

_____

_____

Date to Achieve it: _____

Accountable Person: _____

Notes:

_____

_____

_____

_____

_____

_____

_____

_____

Chapter 18

212° Trading/Investment Systems Designing

What are Systems?

Systems are designed in the form of "Set of Rules."

What is a Trading System?

A Trading System is a set of rules for Buying a Stock or a Commodity, where there is no emotional value in the decision making, similar to a manual car, where there is a concept of A B C – Accelerator, Brake, and Clutch, and there are gears that are to be opted as per the different speed limits; this is how it is driven. Similarly, the purpose of the trading system is to have a certain set of rules to trade and Invest. Be it a day trader, short-term, positional, long-term or micro- minute trader, the trade system is essential to proceed and excel in the world of trading.

"The Biggest Enemy in Trading is you – Yourself."

Trading Systems are generally what we say at Turtle Wealth – the basic function of trading; the way you set your emotional quotient aside while taking a trade decision. This is because an individual is bombarded with news and information sourced through:

- News Papers
- News Channels

- Brokers' Recommendations
- Friends' Recommendations
- Social Media Recommendations

In this way, it is very hard to do anything which is strategically right, and thus, one needs a trading system.

Some Characteristics of 212° Trading Systems:

- Trading strategies are based on a simple universal law that all of us can learn and earn
- No one knows how HIGH and LOW a market or stock will go; we generally believe that people know, but they just pretend to know, because, if they would have really known, they wouldn't have revealed it and have rather encashed it by becoming a millionaire!
- 212° Traders buy based on strength and sell based on weakness
- Using "Common Sense" is not a good way to judge or trade in markets
- Losses are the cost of doing a trading business. No one can be right and make money all the time
- You must take out your emotional content out of yourself like 212° system Traders understand and accept that ***"They Know nothing about Markets and they are the dumbest, yet the most disciplined people in the crowd"***
- Trading Strategies don't give high success ratios. If an individual is right 30–40% of the times, he holds the power to make much more than being 90% right, till the time he knows where to stick and when to exit
- The greatest thing about the trading strategies is that one is not required to remain updated with

anything like demand and supply, sales, profits or any guidance. If the Market is going up – you Buy and still, if it rises, you resist yourself from booking the profits and just keep the happy loss in place. If the market goes in the opposite direction, then exit and take a short position
- Trading Strategies are simple; however, adhering to them is the toughest thing to do
- If a Person Purchases 50 Lottery tickets each week, the probability of him winning the Jackpot can be said to be once in 5000 years
- "You are here to make money, where there are predefined rules, which if not adhered to, may result in your bankruptcy." – from Movie 21
- **One should have "Airplane Pilot Approach"** – Pilots don't plan after they take off the flight or any time during the flight. Everything is pre- decided. Similarly, in the trading system, everything such as stop loss, trades and risk exposure are to be decided before market opens, as post the market opening, an individual would tend to take emotional decisions. Thus, the trading system leads an individual to plan everything in advance, and he can take actions when the market opens. We, at turtle, spare nearly 30 minute *only* for price watch. Incredible, isn't it?

Bad News: I am not going to give anyone a readymade trading system here. By the passage of time, I have understood that trading systems are the reflection of an individual's personality and his trading approach. I prefer such trading systems that hold more of a positional trading approach with an average number of trades of nearly 2–3 times a month, where I don't even have to keep a regular watch at the markets and hold a moderate risk vs. reward ratio with a leverage ratio of 1:3.

A friend of mine follows a Zen-type approach and undergoes very fewer trades in a year, while on the other hand, the other friend of mine is very aggressive in trading and prefers doing only intraday transactions and stays very active in terms of observing the market actions and reactions.

All 3 of us are doing reasonably good with our respective trading and investing approaches, thus, through this, we can rationally say that no system is the best or the worst in the world, as it is completely a reflection of an individual's personality.

But there are some common Rules of Designing a Trading System that should be taken into consideration:

1. **It should have a Module of "Unlimited Profits and Limited Losses:"** I have designed nearly 500 trading systems till now; I am running 5 best systems today – all my systems which gave me heavy losses, where the systems which gave me limited profit, limited losses, or unlimited losses and limited profits. A system which has a clear vision of risk, does not hold any profit target and ensures trailing the stop losses, is the best system on the earth and a holy grail in my opinion.
2. **It should be Unbelievably Simple:** We at Turtle embrace the thought process of Apple brand, as every strategy we make is aimed to be insanely simple. Such strategy can also be called an indicator – One simple Idea followed by rigorous money management and high level of discipline.

If you can teach your trading/ investment strategies to even a teenager, then it can be considered an appropriate strategy.

If a system includes numerous different types of indicators, it might sound great at the time of making the strategy, but believe me, practically it will fail to work.

3. **It should be Boring:** Trading/Investment strategy must be extremely boring; the hardest thing in trading is not having anything to do when the trades are rightly placed – be it long or short. If the trading strategy is full of excitement and thrill, it means that it holds the capacity of digging a grave for your money. A few days ago, a client asked me to design an exciting trading system that could be enjoyed every day. His criterion was that it should have some thrill in it and should be fun to play with. I answered by giving him the address of MGM – Las Vegas.

4. **It should be Perfectly Backtested:** when one makes a Trading Strategy, it must be back tested for at least 5+ years. To assure the resistance of the system against all the market conditions, it is essential that all the phases of bull, bear markets and sideways markets are passed during the testing period.

Backtesting Consists of Average profit, average DD, delta required (Capital required), turtle score, etc.

A detailed description of backtesting has been provided in the backtesting chapter.

5. **It should have a position for 365 Days:** Many trading systems seek for a specific opportunity in future, while as per 212° Trading Approach, the opportunities are uncertain. Thus, one needs to hold positions for any condition – be it long or short.

The market acts in 3 ways: up, down and sideways. Since it is unknown that which way the market would lead, it is essential that the trading system should hold a stop and reverse thought process. These days, the majority of the analysts give advice on exiting from the buying positions, owing to the adverse market conditions. My question here is, "Why can't one opt for a short position?" Here, the longstanding thought process of being the long-term buyers comes into being – they never short, as they are not sure which way the market will head, thus, most of the trading systems should have stop and reverse thought process. As a rule, in Trading Systems at Turtle, we like systems which have round-the-Year Positions.

6. **It Should Answer 7 Questions Perfectly:** The 7 Questions which have been described in detail in the previous chapters.

Summary & Learnings:

- It's very important to Design a Trading/Investment System
- Systems should be sophisticatedly simple to understand
- Airplane Pilot Approach is very important

3 Action Steps to be taken from this Chapter:

1. Action Steps:

_____

_____

Date to Achieve it: _____

Accountable Person: _____

2. Action Steps:

_____

_____

Date to Achieve it: _____

Accountable Person: _____

3. Action Steps:

_____

_____

Date to Achieve it: _____

Accountable Person: _____

Notes:

_____

_____

_____

_____

_____

_____

_____

Chapter 19

212° System Backtesting

"I would never Trade on any System if I have not back tested the data with at least 3 recent cycles of markets."

What is Backtesting? Supposedly Mr. A intends to hire a personnel for the post of a CEO for his company, won't he check the candidate's background? He would also check his/her performance and decisions in the favorable and unfavorable times, his/her qualification, and experience etc. Only after completing such scrutiny, one would hire the candidate, right?

In today's world, we call it a resume. Similarly, in order to access data in advance for the stocks we are going to invest/trade in, we require a resume for the trading systems as well. Thus, even in the trading system, we check everything that has happened in the past, and we take all the decisions accordingly. If we fail to check the background and recruit someone, it can prove to be the worst decision and could cost the company both its goodwill as well as profits. Likewise, in trading, without back testing, one could risk a huge loss of capital.

"Backtesting is like a Backbone for a system; it is very hard and boring to execute but eventually without it, all systems are just conversations."

In my whole trading career, I have traded with several systems, and a lot of times, I have faced losses due to poor back testing or no back testing. Earlier, there were no technical software for backtesting, and even if there were, they were unduly expensive. Therefore, I used to collect the data manually from the exchange website in the excel sheet for making the systems. While today, we are well equipped with fast backtesting modules that could make it easy for us to perform. However, I still believe manual backtesting is essential to attain the requisite accuracy.

We have a very clear approach No Backtesting = **"No"** to any system, in this regard, there are a lot of myths such as:

- Won't Market behave the same way as it behaved during the backtesting?
- Aren't backtesting modules old? Wouldn't they fail to work in the current market conditions?
- Backtesting is a Lengthy process; I believe to trade and conclude by myself

All of these thoughts do not let us stick to a system for a long time, as when we backtest any system, i.e., for trading or Investment, we understand the following:

1. Profit and Loss of the System
2. Money Management is required for sticking to the systems
3. What type of market does the system works in or doesn't work
4. What are the maximum drawdowns of the systems
5. Suitability of the system against the type of trading – Stock/Index/Commodity/Currency

As one of the great traders has quoted, ***"There is a Probability that the system fails to perform well in real-time trading even after having it found to be unobjectionable during back testing. But there is 100% guarantee that if it performs badly*** *during backtesting, then it is going to be bad in real-time trading as well."*

Characteristics of Backtesting:

The Time frame of backtesting:

I generally believe one should have a time frame of minimum 5 years or 3 cycles, i.e., bull cycle, bear cycle and a sideways cycle for back testing. If one makes a system and considers a period of Bull Run in 2005–07 or 2013–15, it will always show a good return, but if he backtests it in all the 3 cycles of back testing the realistic expected returns could be derived.

Manual or Automated:

Frankly speaking, manually feeding the data is the actual way to backtest the system. Also, manual punching of order in excel would keep us posted with the manner the system is performing. It will also help us sense the series where the stop loss is triggered and the series of profitable trades.

2 Important data required in back testing:

1. Drawdown:

It is calculated from any day if you invest in the system of what can be the highest drawdown from the peak of the equity curve, not month to month or year to year.

2. Turtle Score:

The term turtle score is derived from the fact that it is implemented in our company for checking the health of the system, i.e., whether the system is healthy enough to be employed for trading or not.

Turtle Score = Annual ROI%/Maximum Drawdown%

If the Turtle Score is above 1 in the index and above 2 in stocks, it indicates that it is a decent system; the higher the turtle score, the better the system.

3. No. of Trades:

The number of Trades is as important as profits and losses; they directly influence the total returns of the system. I have come across many systems that can give extremely good returns, but they hold more than 350–400 trades in a year. Thus, the execution of such number of trades increases the cost. Hence the profitability is influenced.

The cost of trade increases as the number of trades increase with the following factors:

- Brokerage
- Govt. Taxes
- Impact Cost
- Trade Mistake Cost
- Physiological ups and downs, i.e., cost of emotions

Over the period, I have a gained a sense of making such systems that involve the least number of trades. The 2 types of systems that I trade are the trend following systems that hold a positional view with an average of 12 trades in a year; the second one is the Turtle trading systems which hold nearly 24 trades in a year.

When I mentor Traders, I give them a substantial level of **"Wealth Work"** – like Home Work – for Backtesting. 95% of them fail to complete it. The only reason is the fact that they get bored as they keep getting distracted by calculating profit and loss in between; they give up in between by stating that the system won't work. As per my experience, there are only 5% who are able to backtest religiously and they are the only ones who could excel in Trading/Investing, because if some one is bored doing backtesting itself, how is he going to trade in real?

I understand that the high-frequency traders have a high number of trades in the system, but I can assure you that after attaining a substantial understanding, one will realize that it is not about the number of trades, it all about one's comfort level in trading. If one can reasonably relate his system with the above-described features, then it can be stated that he has gained an in-depth understanding of the system in order to be a *212°: The Complete Trader*.

Summary & Learnings:

- No Backtesting means No Trade
- Backtesting is like a Referral Check
- Turtle Score should be 1+
- Lesser number of Trades can lead to a better system

3 Action Steps to be taken from this Chapter:

1. Action Steps:

_____

_____

Date to Achieve it: _____

Accountable Person: _____

2. Action Steps:

_____

_____

Date to Achieve it: _____

Accountable Person: _____

3. Action Steps:

_____

_____

Date to Achieve it: _____

Accountable Person: _____

Notes:

_____
_____
_____
_____
_____
_____
_____
_____

Chapter 20

The 3 Important C's for Trading/Investing

"Continuous Learning from the masters is the Secret Key to become a Master."

Last year, I attended a Program called "Invest in Yourself" in Flame University – Pune, – India – where all the Stock market masters came and shared their experiences. I was highly motivated by the piece of wisdom shared by Mr. Ramesh Damani – Veteran of Indian Stock Markets. He stated that in order to be Successful in Stock Markets, one needs to have 3 C's in his life (In no formal order):

1. Cash
2. Courage
3. Conviction

Let us understand these 3 C's in brief:

1. Cash:

To start a business, one needs Cash = Liquidity/Money/Investments. Same is the case with Trading/Investment; one needs an Initial Capital to begin. Many new Traders/Investors generally ask me, "How much amount is needed to be a professional Trader?" There is no specific answer to it. I started my career with borrowing money from my father and friends. I had Invested that money in Trading & Investing, while my very good friend started with his savings, but despite everything, the most important point is "Cash." As Mr. Ed Seykota quotes, **"Don't take that much risk that you get broke, but at least take as much risk as the Win is Meaningful."**

Many Amateur Investors and Traders hesitate in entering the market with a small amount of money, as they do not find it enough to make big money out of it. They fail to realize that most of the successful Investors or Traders had begun with only a small amount, which they eventually compounded. They took calculated risks, booked the losses, stuck to the profits, and they made it big – years after years. Therefore, it doesn't matter how much one has; what matters is the manner in which it is used and managed.

We have a rule made by my wife of keeping at least 1 Million in the bank accounts, as it gives immense peace when some venture fails to work or during drawdowns. Many Investors keep 20% cash in hand for future opportunities or for rainy days. As it is not important how much cash you have in markets, but what is important is to place the cash as per the risk appetite so that one is neither underleveraged nor overleveraged. Mr. Warren Buffett, in today's date, keeps $85 Billion in cash, and Apple holds nearly $246 Billion in cash. This justifies that for business or for Trading/Investing, **"Cash is surely a King."**

2. Courage:

There are 2 Types of Courage:

    a. The Courage that is inbuilt

    b. The Courage that comes with Experience and Maturity

The 1st type of Courage in Trading/Investing is more associated with Inheritance, genes or heredity. As one grows, he understands what type of courage is held within him. One can also infer it from observing the family background. My family had always been defensive in risk-taking, thus I have inherited such defensive attitude from my parents towards money.

The 2nd Type of Courage is attained after gaining a significant amount of understanding of a business or process, and thereby, become confident day by day. Even a small success assists in building more and more Courage. Over the passage of time, I started taking huge risks – Calculated, of course – which no one in my family had even taken, but it came with maturity and experience of understanding the process very well. The 2nd type of Courage is generally the Result-Oriented Courage.

Most of the Investors are very skeptic about investing or Trading in Derivatives/Commodities, or the mass has a fear of investing in the stock market. The crux over here is that they have not understood the process, or they have not given adequate time to understand the process and that is the reason for not getting the courage to Invest or Trade.

Courage, as defined by Mr. Ramesh Damani, is when one is aware that the Investment/Trading Idea is remarkable and all odds are in the favour, one should have the courage to **"Truck Load"** the positions, as if he is right. He will surely make immense money and that is how Millionaire/Billionaire Club is enrooted.

I love the lyrics of the song from movie Lagaan, "Har Sant kahe, Sadhu kahe, Sach or Sahash ho jiske mann main, ant main jeet usi ki rahe (All Saints & Gurus say, 'One who has 'Truth & Courage,' only he wins in the end.')"

3. Conviction:

A Firmly-held belief or an opinion which is derived from the enormous level of wisdom and experience. Having self-conviction and confidence in the system or theory is the most important element of a Trader or Investor. In markets, everyone proceeds with a different set of theories, different ways and style of trading/Investing, wherein, the conviction is ensured when one knows exactly what is he doing and is confident about it, even if the whole world goes against him.

As Mr. Utpal Sheth had beautifully quoted, **"Your Patience will be tested, but your conviction will be rewarded."**

There are 2 types of Convictions:

a. **Emotional Conviction:** This conviction occurs when one internally feels to buy, hold or sell the Trade/ Investment – be it inner voice or external voice. Emotional conviction is more relevant while the decision is being taken for the investment. For example, when I understood Gillette as a business, I got convinced emotionally of having it in my Investment Portfolio, with a simple logic of monopoly and great management; it was my Emotional Conviction about the Stock.

b. **Logical Conviction:** This conviction comes from Logic, Data, and Systems to hold on to a trade. I had a recent trade of Long S&P 500 Futures, where the whole world was very pessimistic about Mr. Donald Trump being elected as a president, and the so-called Market Gurus were expecting the market to collapse heavily if Mr. Donald Trump was elected. I had a Long position in S&P 500 at 2000 – with 1800 as Happy Loss. Mr. Donald Trump got elected, but I didn't exit my LONG Position as I had a conviction on my systems and readings. The world is shocked to see S&P 500 today at 2300 A.T.H. (All-Time High); it can be said to be one of the toughest conviction trades of my life.

I have applied one rule: to Listen to Emotional Conviction at the time of Investing and Logical Conviction at the time of Trading.

Conviction is highly tested when markets are not performing well, or when all the implemented ideas are not working. Most of the traders and investors quit at this point of time and start doing something else. I had done a review about the best traders and investors in India. The most common facts in them were: they were in markets from 1980–1990, and they are still in the markets, surpassing all Bull, Bear and Pig phases within this passage of time, but their convictions made them stick to their seats; there are times when despite having a Right System, Methodology, Research Analyst, Cash and Courage Luck doesn't work, and only during that tough time, the **"CONVICTION"** of an individual is tested. So, let me ask you one question:

"If the market does not perform for next 5 Years, do you hold the conviction of staying in the markets?"

If the answer is YES: Trading and Investing is for you.

Summary & Learnings:

- Cash, Courage, and Conviction collectively make a *212°: The Complete Trader*
- Courage comes with Maturity and Experience
- It's not about how much money one has; it's about where one invests that money
- Emotional Conviction is for Investing; Logical Conviction is for Trading

3 Action Steps to be taken from this Chapter:

1. Action Steps:

_____

_____

Date to Achieve it: _____

Accountable Person: _____

2. Action Steps:

_____

_____

Date to Achieve it: _____

Accountable Person: _____

3. Action Steps:

_____

_____

Date to Achieve it: _____

Accountable Person: _____

Notes:

_____

_____

_____

_____

_____

_____

_____

Chapter 21

212° The Spiritual Trader

Spirituality and Trading/Investing are highly interrelated. Without Spirituality, a Trader or an Investor is shallow. One may think of any great trader, businessman or Investor – they would have linked themselves somewhere at some point in time with spirituality. I felt my connection with spirituality when we had a boys' trip to Saputara – Hill station in Southern Gujarat, India – and my friend Tejas introduced Spirituality to me. After understanding the Spiritual laws in detail, I found a complete change in myself as a person, and such changes were also reflected in my Trading & Investing as well.

Spirituality is never bound to any specific religion, caste or creed; it can be followed through any of the holy scripts Bhagavadgita, the Holly Bible, Upanishads, Vedas or Quran-e-Sharif etc. Each one of those focus on defining the Universal Principles, stating that there exists a supreme power. The best part is that they are so profound that, if we follow them, we don't need anything else. However, we generally fail to do that.

During this transition phase of Spirituality, I heard the podcast of Mr. Joel Osteen – Pastor from Lakewood Church and listening to his podcast changed my thought process regarding life, money and the God.

I would share with you the 11 Profound Spiritual Financial Principles that will uplift your Trading and Investing MOJO.

1. Keep God in the First Place:

When we start keeping God in the first place before taking any decision on Investing or Trading we tend to get hints in the form of feeling confident towards any situation, in the form of intuitions – that is the God's voice within us. Many times, we listen to our instant gratification or greed, and we make decisions without listening to our inner self; some external force will restrain us from doing so. Those are the signals given by God to convey that the decision is not right. However, this is only possible if we prioritize and place him in the foremost position in the decision making.

One of my friends once came with a strategy that apparently looked very lucrative as it promised higher returns, and my flesh forced me to go for it. I left it to God and asked for his permission to proceed, he gave me 3 signals of not going ahead with that deal for some reason or the other, but however, I failed to pick the hints and eventually, the total investment turned out to be a complete loss.

So how can one connect to God and keep him in the first place? Here are some of the ways through which one can do that:

a. Meditate:

Wake up at 4 AM – that is the time when God is free to listen to us, as almost all the living beings are sleeping, and it's the time where there is no technological distraction as no one will disturb us via WhatsApp or Facebook. Sit silently, closing the eyes for 15 minutes. It will seem tough for initial 21 days, but thereafter, one will feel a divine energy around him that would converse with him, and most of the decisions he takes in that span of time will result in the right to riches.

One Day in that solitude: I had a feeling that market was going to shoot with a V-shape recovery. On that morning, I went to the office and told my Colleague Vibhati; at that point of juncture, everyone refused to believe me; nevertheless, owing to the market position in the middle of Greece War news, the expected depression in China, it was hard to believe. To be honest, even I failed to believe it, but it turned out to be a reality within a span of exactly one month. I am not advising anyone to take financial tips from it, but this is true that when ours' and god's decisions collide; there is always a win-win situation in long run.

So, the next time in confusion and lack of confidence, don't take spontaneous decisions. I would advise rather sleep over it and wait for the next day's meeting with God at 4 AM. ask and express all the dilemmas to him; he will surely provide some signals or intuitions for you to undertake a correct decision.

b. Write Gratitude Letters

Gratitude letters is a practice that I learned from the movie named "The Secret", and till date, I write every day to God, thanking him for whatever he has bestowed on us and thanking him in advance for whatever that has been asked from the God.

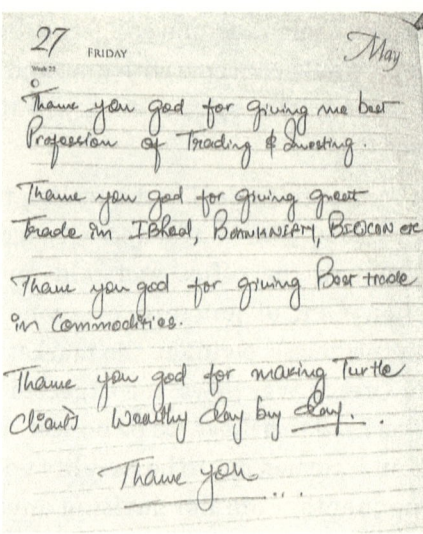

This is a picture from my Gratitude Diary, where I am thanking God for everything he has already granted me or he would grant me in future.

So, when you get a great trade, thank him. If you are getting DD, still, thank him for getting the best trades in future.

Every day, after meditation, reserve your 5 minutes to write a gratitude letter to the God, to thank him for everything.

So, every morning you are prioritizing the God at first place in your life, before anything else.

2. God's Plans Are Better than Ours:

Jeremiah 29:11 "For I know the plans I have for you," declares the Lord, "Plans to prosper you and not to harm you, plans to give you hope and a future."

We have our desires, plans, goals, and everything. When we achieve those, we are happy and satisfied, and we tend to believe it's a result of our smartness and hard work, while on the other hand, when we fail to do so, we blame it on the God. I believe that when our plans are not going in the right direction, it's something big and better that has been planned for us, which is beyond our imagination and would surprise us.

When we had a series of drawdowns in our System in Index and Commodities, all of my dreams and goals of that period of time got sunk; I had completely lost all my hopes, however, I didn't give up and I made all-time high profits in derivatives in the next 3 months, which was beyond my imagination.

When a lady is expecting, she has to go through a sequence of pain before delivering a baby, yet, if asked post- delivery, will she complain about the pain or will she praise the gift of the God in the form of a baby? Of course, she would praise, right? Similar is the case with trading and investing. We need to understand that when things are not going our way, God is preparing something big for us, **either in the form of learning or in the form of earning**.

The systems I have developed till today – none of those had been developed in the good times; all were developed because of a huge DD in the previous system or something wrong that had happened. In hindsight, all my systems in today's date are the results of the things which didn't go well

those were the plans of the God and were indeed better than mine.

In 2010, I made a system and I lost almost all the saving I had; I thought I was finished, but if I peek into the past today, I would say I got the biggest lesson of my life in the form of never trading in a system which has "Limited Profits and Limited Losses." Maybe, at that juncture, it was one of the biggest lessons I should have learned to earn big in the coming time.

So, let us understand it this way- if we win our way, we are happy, but when we lose, we should be happier with something big and better is being planned for us. Simply, if we get a winning trade, we are happy, but when times are tough, believe that biggest trade is on the way!

If you see this picture carefully, God is asking a toy from the kid – the one that she loves the most – in exchange for something which the girl's mind might not have conceived and imagined.

"Tougher times are for the Lucky People chosen by God to grow and excel."

3. Be an Owl:

Every goddess has a ride on which she travels. Laxmiji is the goddess of wealth in Hindu mythology and her ride is an owl. Owl has the power of visibility in the dark, and almost everyone fails to do so. Similarly, to be a *212°: The Complete Trader/* investor, one needs to capitalize an opportunity which is not visible to others.

Likewise, if one is investing where the mass invests, there is a very less probability of getting great returns on investments. We have to think, act and execute differently to be an Owl. Following are the 5 steps to be an Owl Trader/Investor:

1. Trade the things which are highly popular, invest in the things which are least popular
2. Very few people understand the power of compounding, and out of them, only limited people are able to avail that power. We need to have the patience to understand the power of compounding
3. Take short positions, 98% Traders or Investors tend to take only long positions. They fail to understand the power of taking the short positions during the unfavorable market conditions
4. Read books; meet great Investors/Traders, very few people do it
5. Have the courage to hold onto profits and exit in losses

4. We don't have any control over the outcome:

When we do a trade, we stick to the screen; we keep watching fluctuation in the prices; we keep reviewing our portfolio – twice and even more in a day – but we should ask a question to ourselves that "Do we really have any control on the outcomes?" The answer is NO. We can do our best at the task, but the outcome can be either a Win or a Loss. While Trading/Investing, our only Focus should be- "Are we following our systems?" Are we doing adequate money management and ensuring enjoyment during the process etc., or is our focus only on the outcomes that we could get from the actions?

कर्मण्येवाधिकारस्ते मा फलेषु कदाचन।
मा कर्मफलहेतुर्भूर्मा ते सङ्गोऽस्त्वकर्मणि॥ २-४७

"KarmanyeVaadhikaraste Ma Phaleshu Kadaachana, Ma Karma PhalahetuBhurma Tey SangostvaAkarmani."

The art lies in walking the tightrope and enjoying it. If the individual walking the tightrope gets scared or becomes too excited, he will certainly fall. The trick to his success is ensuring that he enjoys while he walks to reach the other end successfully. In our organisation Turtle wealth, we truly believe and practice this notion.

Below are the founders of Turtle Wealth, where we have declared GOD as the **"Chief Result Officer,"** because at the end of the day, results are never in our hands; they are only the actions that could be controlled by us. So why should we be concerned about the results? We should rather be focussed on the betterment of our actions and the manner in which we may improve them day by day. Moreover, we should analyse whether we are learning from our mistakes and whether we are humble enough to realize that whatever we have gained is because of our partnership with the God.

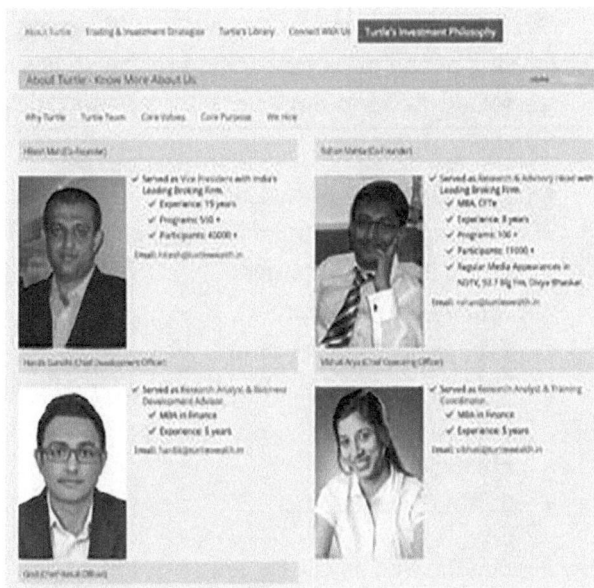

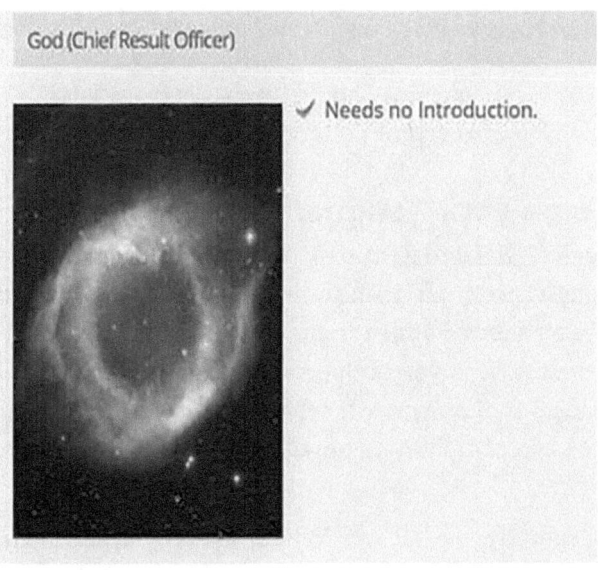

- Once we understand this, we would surely stop looking at the price by sticking to the screens and we would develop our control over the following things:
  * Adhering to our System
  * Trading or investing with right principles
  * Being 100% Disciplined
  * Money Management
  * Emotional Management
  * Taking Knowledge – Reading and Meeting Great People
  * Hiring a Mentor
  * Taking Training etc.

When we made the God as our Chief Result officer, we were more focused on our actions. The pressure of achieving results drained day by day, and whatever result came, either profit or loss, we just asked only 2 questions to ourselves:

1. What learning should we derive from this?
2. How to become better than what we were Yesterday?

5. Tame your Tongue:
Proverb 1428: I will do exactly what you are saying.

Joel Osteen has mentioned it many times: **"You don't need any enemy; your tongue does it for you."** As a Trader or Investor, it is very important to focus on what are we uttering out of our mouth, whether it is optimistic, nagging or we keep complaining about what we have and what we don't?

Generally, we all are YO-YO Traders, where, when a trade goes right and we make money, we believe it has happened because of us, but once the trade fails to work, we start blaming the markets, the conditions, the event, the broker and sometimes even our spouse and kids. We can't afford to be YO-YO Happy sometimes; sad sometimes. We must learn to tame our tongue in terms of the things which we intend, and not the things which we don't really mean. However, our flesh forces us to do so and we keep blaming other factors for our losses in the trade such as:

- The Market is never in my favour
- My stop losses always trigger
- Whatever I buy, trades always go down
- My Broker or Advisor is not good
- I am not Lucky, and so on.

"What we speak comes into being." – Bhagwad Gita

We should have a huge amount of control on what we speak, as we never know when they'll turn out to be true. It implies on what we listen as well, as it gets stored in our subconscious mind. Train your tongue to talk only about wealth, prosperity, happiness and other great things, even during the unfavourable situations. When I lost everything in 2010, my friend asked me if I am repenting for what I did, and my answer was, "I believe this will be the biggest breakthrough for my future." I could have said yes, and could have blamed it on the markets, my bad luck, but taming the tongue is a magic trick to be the *212°: The Complete Trader*.

This chart will help you with taming your tongue in different situations.

What We Speak	What Should We Speak
Market is not performing well	Market is market; it's the way we trade or invest that makes the difference
Here, everyone makes losses	I don't have any control on losses and profits. I only focus on my systems
No one has earned from market	There are many people who have earned remarkably from market and we need to learn from them
It is very risky	We need to do adequate risk management
I did a big mistake	I will learn from my mistakes and will grow better day by day
I want to get rich fast	I want to be wealthy, Step by Step
I don't like losses	Losses are a part of business; they are inevitable and we need to be prepared for it

6. This Too Shall Pass

This is a Persian Proverb and the best message that could be conveyed to mankind; it has helped me a lot in my career as a trader, investor, and entrepreneur.

This goes with a story of a king who asked the people of the kingdom to give him a secret that would prove to be useful, whenever he faces any tough time. Many people tried and failed till a wise man came and gave a box to the king by taking a promise that he would open the box, only when he is in a real trouble. The king agreed to it. After some years, his kingdom was attacked by his rivals, and he was about to lose his kingdom. At that time, he opened the box and he found a note in it with a message stating: "This too shall pass." The king got motivated and won the war. When he came home, he was praised by the people of the kingdom and he read the message again that stated "This too shall pass." He did not let the success rule his head as he understood that like other things, even this praise and prosperity is also temporary.

"In Life, Everything is Temporary." - Imam Ali

Similar is the case with trading/Investing as well. When we are going through good times and everything is working our way, there exists the highest probability of bearing losses. This is because we generally get carried away and take bets with high leverage, do trades for fun, undergo trades that are not in our systems and we get the biggest hit. The same way when things are not going well, the market is very choppy with the highest level of drawdowns. That is the time, where if we stay patient, we may have the highest probability of hitting the biggest trade, but most of us exit from our system during that phase only. If we understand

This Shall Too Pass Manifesto, we will neither get carried away nor get demotivated while being a trader/investor.

7. Giving Back Before You Have Even Earned:

Once I went to meet my friend Abhishek Kamdar at his office and we were having a market-related conversation; in the middle of it, his father also joined. I generally have a habit of asking such senior personalities about their secrets of life and he was kind enough to share his secret.

He told me the Biggest Secret to creating wealth is to "Make GOD as the Partner," i.e., official Partner; give him a partnership in your Trading/Investing or Business and the percentage can range from 1% to any percent as per your wish and devotion. I was thrilled upon listening to this. I asked him how it helps; he told me that when you make someone a partner, he is linked with your profits and losses, and when you make God as your partner, there won't be a loss; there will be only profits. I asked how that was possible; he answered that when the God is at your side, he will never allow you to take wrong steps, and you will be saved from doing the wrong things. I got that on the 1st Strike!

I asked him what happens to the profit share of the God? Where do I send? He replied, "Give it to the people who need it, in terms of Education, Health or any other form of assistance that is required." Trust me, from that day, I have made god as a partner in my Personal Wealth as well as Turtle Wealth, and I have observed that I have been saved from a lot of mishaps, which could have occurred if the God was not my Partner.

If we observe the billionaires across the globe, be it Mr. Warren Buffett, Mr. Bill Gates, Mr. Azim Premji, Mr. Narayan Murthy or Mr. Rakesh Jhunjhunwala, all are the legendary examples for us to know that "Nobody in the world has ever become poor by giving." Rather, the rule of Universe states that, "The More you give, the more you get; the faster you give, the faster you receive."

8. Flesh vs. Spirit

In Trading and life, there is a great fight between Flesh and Spirit, where Flesh asks us to do the things which we like, but subconsciously we are aware of the fact that they will lead us nowhere such as no exercising, no reading, excessive spending and also the lack of discipline while trading/ investing. All these things attract us, but internally, we are aware that we will not attain any result out of it. While, doing exercise, reading every day and following the systems might seem to be very tough initially, but they can provide substantial results eventually.

In Trading and Investing, Flesh vs. Spirit hold great importance. Flesh is generally the Saturn inside us while Spirit is the God inside us; it completely depends on us that to whom we are going to listen more, as it will define our future ahead. The more we start listening to Spirit, the wealthier, healthier and more prosperous we would become.

So, it begins with doing the right things – paying taxes on time, paying all the other dues in time, not doing any double-dealing of money, etc. Let me give you an example: Some years ago, due to some back-office mistake, my Demat account was credited with 1000 Shares of Tata Consultancy Services quoting somewhere around 1090 INR per share, i.e., a total of. 10,90,000 INR. I was shocked as I saw the transaction in my Demat account. Initially, my Flesh alleged that I am very lucky; I can use this to buy my Dream House and even a Car, but my Spirit intervened and said that it is not right; it is not my money, so I should return it back. After a day of fight between Flesh and Spirit, I called the broker and gave back the shares. Initially, I was not very happy, but I believe what I am today is only because of that decision.

When we started Turtle, we had some options of taking fees in cash for evading tax, but we took the option of taking all Income in cheque ; it was very hard initially, but after Demonetization, it seems to be the best decision we could have ever taken.

Spirit is painful, as its results are late, but they are guaranteed to be extraordinary, while on the other hand, making decisions by listening to flesh is fun, its results are also good initially, but in long run, they prove to be futile.

The actions taken by listening to the directions given by flesh give DEBIT in our Life Account, whereas the actions that are taken in directions ushered by the Spirit give CREDIT in our Life Account.

Differentiating between Flesh and Spirit in Trading and Investing:

Flesh	Spirit
Make Quick Rich Trades	Follow the right Path
Break Discipline	Follow it somehow, no matter what
Do not Take knowledge, You are already full of knowledge	Take knowledge; it is the key to success
I will never book loss; I don't need Stop Loss	Losses are part of business; I have to accept it.
I will never take short positions	Short positions are as important as taking long positions
Trade for fun and excitement	Trade as a business with seriousness
I don't need a mentor	Behind Every Successful trader, there is a Mentor
Big losses—Small Profits Trades	Big Profits—Small Losses Trades only

As a Trader and Investor, one must decide whether he wants to adhere to Flesh or Spirit, and once he starts listening only to his Spirit, he is already a *212°: The Complete Trader*.

9. God Too took a lot of Pain to be God!

I am a Spiritual Person. I follow all Gods and all religions where I get Serenity; I have read about nearly all gods, which have been accepted by the people across the globe, and I found that each one of them had taken a lot of pain before they were crowned as God, be it:

- Mahavira
- Buddha
- Rama
- Allah's Messengers
- Krishna
- Jesus
- Sai Baba
- Guru Nanakji

All of them were betrayed; they left their kingdoms, and there were times when they were standing alone, with no one at their side, yet they never left their path of doing the righteous things for people around the world. In Trading and Investing too, it is going to be painful; it is not going to be as smooth as it is depicted by so many fund Managers and financial planners, as there will be times when there will be situations such as:

- High Drawdowns
- Market not favouring your system
- Mistakes adding to the Pain

- Your stocks, systems or market not giving a return for many years, and you might think of giving up on it

A time would come when no one would support us, but with adequate internal belief, and along with the rigorous follow up of the book, I can claim it with surety that we are on the right path to SUCCESS already.

10. Achieving the Degree of SERENITY

Serenity is **"The absence of mental stress or anxiety"** – a place where there is no profit or loss; it's a complete bliss – the addition of Spirituality in Trading and Investing takes you to the zone of Serenity.

It takes some decades to reach this stage of Serenity, but once it is attained, it's the money that works for you and not the other way around.

In the Holy book Bhagwat Gita, Serenity is defined as being a **"Karma Yogi."** Karma yogi is the one whose emotions do not change as per the outcomes of the actions; rather, they always remain the same – be it good times or bad. If such a zone is attained, it's the serenity.

Serenity is the state of knowing not to worry about the outcome; rather, it is about focusing on the actions, learning from the mistakes and not repeating them; the actions that are taken become so important that we are not concerned with what the results turn out to be.

Let's us understand this with an example – we make a system or a procedure; we invest or trade according to that system, irrespective of whether the system is formed on the basis of technical or fundamental research. However, the worth of system is decided from the results we attain from it, not from the actions we had taken for making that system. If we only focus on the results of any system or a procedure, there is the highest probability that, in a short time, we will stop using the system, and we will start focusing on some other system. Moreover, any system that we find, the pain will still be the same, as the focus is only on the result and not on the actions. As a Trader or Investor, we need to understand very clearly, that only actions are in our control – and not the results so why to worry about whether we get profit or loss till:

- Our Systems have Big Profits and Small Loss
- Our Risk Management is in place
- We are 100% Disciplined
- We are planning even for the worst before entering the trade
- We are not taking any emotional call and following what our system is saying

I met a trader in the USA who visits his broker's office only once in a year, he has delegated his trading system to the broker, and he has compounded his wealth to a marvelous level. Just because he is completely in serenity, he told his broker to only follow the system and not to focus on profit or loss.

I manage a fund of an HNI – High Networth Individual who came to visit me with his concerns pertaining to reduced returns, and I raised a question to him that where was he when the returns were very high. To which he answered that at that time he was satisfied and content, and now he is not. I asked him again whether I had changed my procedure of trading/investing. He shook his head. I asked then why was he worried. Only through this conversation,

I inferred that he was completely concerned with the Profit and Loss and not the process, and that was the reason of him facing lack of endurance and anxiety.

Even the biggest organizations or the billionaires across the globe are never concerned about the results, rather they lay their meticulous focus on the process itself.

"The Day we shift our focus from profits and losses to the actions; that would be the day when we have achieved Serenity."

How to Achieve Serenity?

- Wake up at 4 am and Meditate
- Don't Over Expect the returns
- Don't get too much excited when you win or get too much upset when you lose
- Read – Read & Read
- Give Back whatever you have earned
- Don't focus on Results; focus on the Actions

I am sure that, after doing all of these, you will attain the zone of Serenity for being a *212°: The Complete Trader*.

Summary & Learnings:

- Spirituality ensures Serenity
- Make the GOD as your Chief Result Officer
- Giving back even what is not earned yet

3 Action Steps to be taken from this Chapter:

1. Action Steps:

_____

_____

Date to Achieve it: _____

Accountable Person: _____

2. Action Steps:

_____

_____

Date to Achieve it: _____

Accountable Person: _____

3. Action Steps:

_____

_____

Date to Achieve it: _____

Accountable Person: _____

Notes:

_____

_____

_____

_____

_____

_____

_____

_____

Chapter 22

The Discipline Factor

"Pain of Regret or Pain of Discipline?"

The word trading apparently begins with **"T"** but it starts with the letter **"D"** where D stands for "Discipline" I have interviewed, read, met and traded with most of the best traders in the world and as per all of them, the most important thing is **"Discipline."** It is very easy to say but extremely hard to maintain. It's not only significant in trading or investing; it is equally important in the personal life or other businesses. Radical discipline is mandatory in order to attain the desired success.

Here, the term discipline does not refer to the stringent rules and regulations; they are being referred as the basic self-restraints that are generally known by everyone, but are hardly followed.

2 Axioms that I admire for disciplines are:

a. **"We don't have to be smarter than others; we have to be more disciplined than others."** stated by Mr. Warren Buffett

b. **"The day lust for discipline turns bigger than the love for profit, one will become a real 212°: *The Complete Trader*"**

– Rohan Mehta

I have come across hundreds of traders and investors who were smarter than their co-traders/investors on the street, in terms of:

- Money
- Information
- Infrastructure
- Knowledge, etc.

But as of today, they are out of the markets, as they had lacked the basic discipline required in trading and the market had taken a big price from them.

Discipline has also been numerically proven to be 100% needed, by taking the total of the ranks of alphabets in the term *discipline*:

- **D = 4**
- **I = 9**
- **S = 19**
- **C = 3**
- **I = 9**
- **P = 16**
- **L = 12**
- **I = 9**
- **N = 14**
- **E = 5**
- **Total = 100**

No wonder the total count of discipline came out to be 100; the basic reason is, even after leaving everything aside, if the actions are taken with adequate discipline, then one becomes capable of leaving the smarter, wealthier and more knowledgeable people behind.

It took me more than 10 years to understand the power of discipline; I still struggle in many areas as there still lies a scope of growth in them. However, in trading and investing, I can claim to be 98% disciplined. It is essential to understand the significance of discipline, not only in the arena of work and profession but also in the personal life, then only one can think of becoming a *212°: The Complete Trader*.

Discipline Survey

This is an amazing survey. Let's see how Disciplined are you. Make a choice between the options – a, b or c. One is required to be extremely honest while answering the questions as they hold relatively more relevance:

1. **Are you generally on time where you have to reach or have committed Time?**
   a. Every time
   b. Some Time
   c. Never

2. **Do you have an Exercise/Diet Regime?**
   a. Yes, and I follow
   b. Yes, but I don't follow
   c. No, I don't have

3. **Do you fulfill the commitment given by you to your spouse & Kids?**
   a. Every time
   b. Sometimes
   c. Never

4. **Do you maintain your Accounting and Trading Journal?**
   a. Every time
   b. Sometimes
   c. Never

5. **Do you have a Daily Regime?**
   a. Yes, and I follow
   b. Yes, but I don't follow
   c. No, I don't have

6. **Do you fulfill the commitment given to yourself?**
   a. Every time
   b. Sometimes
   c. Never

7. **How Disciplined are you in your Trading/Investments?**
   a. Highly
   b. Moderate
   c. Not at all

8. **Do you pay your bill/dues on Time?**
   a. Every time
   b. Sometimes
   c. Never

9. **If given Apple or Cake, which one will you eat?**
   a. Apple
   b. Confused
   c. Cake, for sure

10. **Generally, do you break the discipline, just to please someone?**
    a. Never
    b. Sometimes
    c. Every time

Results:

7+ A's = Congratulations, you maintain the top-notch level of Discipline; you have the highest probability to make the most out of being a Trader/Investor; you are generally a Left Brain thinker who thinks Negative first before positive.

You face issues in thinking out of the box, and to be highly open minded, you are generally "Big Profits and Small Losses" Trader; you give very high importance to Money Management. You are suggested to have a Trading Buddy who has more B's; you need to be guided in terms of taking risks and how to think out of the box.

7+ B's = You are in a category where you know everything, but are unable to execute. You are always in the repenting game, generally a "Small Profit–Small Loss" Trader; you are a Whole Brain thinker who analyses Positive and Negative in everything; you are very afraid of what society will say, and care a lot to be an "I know everything Syndrome" person, to be right is more important than making money for you. You are suggested to have a Trading buddy who has more A's, you need a training on how to be rigorously Disciplined.

7+ C's = You are in the High Danger Zone; you are a right brain thinker – super creative, dreamer and visionary, but very poor with Discipline. You are generally a "Big Loss – Small Profits" Trader; you need to change your approach, and there is an urgent requirement for you to have a Mentor, and you need to have 2 Trading Buddies – one with more A's, and one who has more B's in their respective discipline surveys.

For being the best, the following 9 Commandments will help in making you Highly Disciplined.

8 Commandments to be a Highly-Disciplined Trader:

1. 999 Days Rule:

In trading/investing, we make numerous systems by applying permutations, combinations and put the systems on trial, and if they fail to function, we leave them aside – neither a system nor a trading oscillator is always right; they take their own time. Many traders quit the system in between by stating that it is not working adequately and keep hopping from one system to another without patience.

Thus, the rule states that whichever system is introduced by the trader, it should be put on trial for at least 999 days with 100% discipline.

- **Disciplined Entry – Adherence to the system**: After adopting a system, one needs to follow it rigorously, and the investments should be bought and sold strictly as per the system, without entertaining any emotional or rational thought process.
- **Disciplined Exit – As Per System**: After having attained the happy loss, either in the case of buy or short, one needs to exit without being influenced by any of the external forces such as news, TV Analysts, brokers, etc.
- **Disciplined Money Management**: If it has been decided to Trade 1 Contract of S&P 500/ NIFTY/Gold, one is required to maintain the same for 999 days. The 999 days can be said to be nearly 3 years, where even if a mediocre system is adopted religiously, then also, it will prove to be a better performer than Speculating or emotional trading.

2. Trade like the Beggar:

I keep asking this question to everyone, "Who is the most motivated person across the globe?" Different people give different answers, but according to me, the answer is a "Beggar." He gets the highest rate of rejections across all his mark – he hears bad words, but he never gets demotivated; he keeps begging from one target to another to achieve his day-to-day target.

We are much better than beggars; we have a home to live, we have a place to work and money to survive; still, we get depressed and demotivated easily. We keep quitting every now and then assuming that nothing works, but the beggars never give up. If an individual has said NO to them even thrice before, they will still go to him the next time, asking for money, and as per my analysis, a beggar goes to a man at-least for 10 days despite of facing consecutive denial. The man will eventually end up giving him money someday; similar is the case with markets as well.

I trade like a beggar – I can mention this without any shame. Even if 9 of my trades fail to work, I still remain motivated to trade for the 10th time with the same zeal and vigor that I carried during my first trade. If we develop the attitude of beggars while trading and investing, I am sure it can prove to be one of the most motivational commandments of trading ever!

3. Journalizing the Trades:

Journalizing the Trades is one of the most boring but most significant parts of discipline. I realized its importance a few years ago when I began with journalizing all my trades – It acts as a mirror of what is being traded and invested.

Journalizing trades has 2 parts:

1st: Details of Trade Sheet:

a. No.

b. Date

c. Name

d. Buy Rate

e. Sell Rate

f. Quantity

g. Exposure = Total of Quantity*Buy/Sell Rate

h. Commissions

I. P&L

i. Details: trade details, the reason behind booking the trade, or anything good or bad that had happened in association with the trade such as:

   i. Though I met with a loss, I was much disciplined in the trade

   ii. Because of my poor discipline, I booked the profit early and missed the biggest trade

   iii. I didn't exit the Trade and didn't follow my systems

These tactics will enable an individual to stay cautious while making mistakes and even in the case of having attained good results in the last trades.

2nd: Debit the Losses First – This has been a revolutionary technique in which one journalizes his trades and the trades are kept open in his journal. One is required to keep his stop loss in place, i.e., when to exit from the stock and assess the loss figure.

4. Discipline = Delegation

"We are disciplined in being undisciplined."

The best wisdom to follow with radical discipline is to delegate. If an individual designs a system that can be completely delegated to an amateur, it means that his system is 100% mechanical, and it is the sign of being a *212°: The Complete Trader*.

Once the system has been designed, recruit an amateur executor with the basic knowledge of the market and is capable of executing the trade. His duty is restricted to the execution of the trades perfectly as per the system and leave everything else aside. Moreover, he/she should not hold any interest in the profits and losses; that's one of the best ways to be 100% disciplined.

As the teachers find it very hard to teach their own kids, in the same way, it's very hard for a System Creator & Professional Trader to trade with 100% Discipline, as they have emotions linked to the systems. Moreover, this is the biggest black hole, but if the system is delegated, it becomes easier to do the process. In this case, if an individual is a system trader who executes trades with software – without manual trades – it is still advised to have someone who monitors the system.

I had done this 5 years ago and had received exponential results from the same; I have delegated the whole account to my colleague Vibhati, who is highly disciplined, also accompanied by immense integrity. Thus, whenever she finds me doing overleveraged trades, she stops me; she never asks me if the next trade is to be done; she simply trades, and every month, I just review my monthly data of different systems to know the profit and Loss. In India, when we trade, at the end of the day, we get trade confirmations via SMS; I had also shifted those trade confirmations to her number.

"If we Trust our systems, we should Delegate 100%; if we don't, we should not trade at all."

5. Avoiding Quick Rich Formula Trap

I fear a lot from traders who claim their systems generate 100–200–500% return every year; they might have given returns in backtesting, but in actual trading, if such huge returns are attained, then it might be accompanied by a huge risk of blowing up everything.

" Easy profits are accompanied by highest risk."

We all have heard about being **"Quick Rich;"** did we ever hear about being **"Quick Wealthy?"**

Market, Media, and Brokers intend to give an individual many short-term trades, where quick bucks could be grabbed as the mind wants excitement, but we should not get attracted towards such short-term small chunk trades, which do not form a part of our systems and can prove to be hazardous for profits and wealth.

Mr. Charlie Munger once nicely quoted **"It is remarkable how much long-term advantage people like us have got by consistently trying not to be stupid, instead of trying to be very intelligent."** He said almost everything in these 2 lines. To succeed in trading, only if we adhere to our systems, we will get wealthier in comparison to any trader who opts for such Quick Rich Game.

I generally look for the systems that are boring, time-consuming and hold a known risk. Since they hold the probability of making me rich, I genuinely won't mind investing money and time in that system or trade.

My wife Namrata explains this very well, by stating that systems are like a wife with whom one gets bored easily; one does not find them exciting and they are taken for granted. While on the other hand, the trading systems of others are like another women who are found to be more attractive and worth spending time and money. While the real happiness and love are rendered only by wife, opting for another woman can ruin the current life. Thus, the crux of what she meant to convey was that wife and boring- yet efficient systems are the only ways to find happiness and wealth!

6. Living a Disciplined Life

As discussed before, one cannot be a disciplined trader if he is not 100% disciplined in life. Discipline comes from taking care of health, family, kids, and everything. No wonders why Soldiers, Pilots and Army men turn out to be very successful Traders as the 1st thing they are taught in the army is Discipline. One should follow a structured life as discussed in chapter-The Day of *212°: The Complete Trader.*

7. Having a Trading Buddy

Trading/Investing is a long journey. It's very important to have a Trading Buddy in taking decisions; he/she can help you if you are going wrong anywhere. It's better if you have a buddy who holds a different thought process like my Trading buddies are Tejas and Vibhati; Tejas is my Investment buddy and Vibhati is my Trading buddy. The nature of both of them is completely different from that of mine. I still ask them before taking any big decision. In many cases, I have been able to take the majority of my right decisions just because of them; especially the times when I get an urge to break the discipline, it helps me a lot, and maybe because of them, I hold an edge on Trading & Investing. Thus, through my experience, I can claim that one is required to have a trading buddy. The qualities that one can look for while selecting a trading buddy could be:

    a. Trading Buddy should think differently

    b. Trading Buddy should be successful in his personal Trading/Investments

    c. Trading Buddy should be blunt enough to stop you from taking wrong decisions

    d. Trading Buddy should have no bias against you

Before going ahead, please appoint your Trading Buddies Now:

    i. Trading Buddy: _____
    ii. Trading Buddy: _____
    iii. Trading Buddy: _____

Call and tell them, "From today onwards, you are my "Trading Buddy", amongst my official Board of Directors for my Trading and Investments."

8. Goal Card

Design your own Goal Card for 10 years, 5 years, 3 years, 2 years and 1 year and Review it Quarterly. To know where to reach, having a specific way is very important; also, have Goals of developing a Specific Discipline and keeping them:

a. In front of your Working Desk

b. As Mobile Wallpaper

c. As Laptop Wallpaper

d. In Your Bathroom

e. In Places where you Brush, etc., to remind you every time, what are your goals in life.

Summary & Learnings:

- The pain of Discipline is less painful than the pain of regret
- Discipline score says much about us
- Having a Trading Buddy is the key
- Be a Beggar in trading/investing

3 Action Steps to be taken from this Chapter:

1. Action Steps:

_____

_____

Date to Achieve it: _____

Accountable Person: _____

2. Action Steps:

_____

_____

Date to Achieve it: _____

Accountable Person: _____

3. Action Steps:

_____

_____

Date to Achieve it: _____

Accountable Person: _____

Notes:

_____

_____

_____

_____

_____

_____

_____

_____

Chapter 23

10 Qualities to Trade Like Rama & Not Be a Ravana

If we understand Spirituality, the main purpose is to knowing ourselves very well, is to remove odds and focus on the Good and Work on improving them; same is the case in Trading. It is a Journey to remove the odds in us as Human beings and Focus on the best and work on them.

Why do We celebrate **Dussehra** or **Dasara** or **Dashain**? As per Hindu religion, on this day in the Treta Yug, King Rama – also called as Shri Ram, the seventh avatar of

Vishnu – killed Ravana who had abducted Rama's wife Sita to his kingdom of Lanka. Rama, his brother Lakshmana, their follower Hanuman and an army fought a great battle to rescue Sita. The entire narrative is recorded in the epic Ramayana – a Hindu scripture.

Many people perform "Aditya Homa" as a "Shanti Yagna" and recite Sundara Kanda of Srimad Ramayana for 5 days. These Yagna performances are believed to create powerful vibes in the atmosphere of the house and keep the household environment clean and healthy. These rituals are intended to get rid of the 10 bad qualities, which are represented by 10 heads of Ravana as follows:

These 10 bad qualities are also present in a trader or an investor. I will try to illustrate and explain the same to you so that it assists in making you a Rama Trader.

1. Vasana (Lust):

"Lust is generally a Craving for anything which is more than necessary;" this generally happens in Trading or Investing with:

- Lust for: Getting Everything Right
- Lust for: Getting Short Term Profits
- Lust for: Predicting Markets
- Lust for: getting only Multibaggers
- Lust for: finding the Holy Grail Trading Systems
- Lust for: Picking Top & Bottoms

Generally, such Lust make us so tempted that we forget our Real Trading Purpose, i.e., to do the things which are in our hands with perfection in a manner that the market rewards for the other things that are not in our control.

2. Krodha (Anger):

I generally see this in both the Trader & Investor – day in, day out – Even though Duryodhana knew what was right and wrong, he still chose the wrong path, and he was always seen in an angry state, whereas Arjuna was focused towards right deeds, was stable and poised.

As a Trader, if you do not maintain Discipline, if you do Short-Term Instant Gratification Trade, you would never succeed.

The things that are not in your hands such as market fluctuations, news, gap up gap downs should never make you angry, if adequate control over the things which are in your hands are assured.

3. Moha (Attachment):

This is a problem that most of us go through for the entire life, and we need to work on improving it day by day. **"The one who has no Moha, gets more than the one who has."**

- The Attachment of watching price movements daily
- The Attachment of Calculating Profit and Loss
- The Attachment with the Tick of Markets and Fluctuations
- The Attachment for Systems

These Attachments make us a Ravana Trader.

4. Lobha (Greed):

As per my opinion, Greed is essential. If you are not greedy, technically you should not enter Stock Markets. Fixed Deposit is the word for you, but an excess of everything is bad, thus excessive Greed is something which kills a Trader.

Excessive Greed comes during good times, when your conscious mind presumes that nothing can go wrong with you, as the good things that have happened to you – which are consequences of the right steps you had taken – provokes you to take wrong steps such as:

- Not being Physically Fit
- Trading out of the System
- Being Overleveraged
- Believing in people more than your system and mentor
- Trading like a Casino Player

All of these are the traits of a Greedy Person that would always make a Ravana Trader.

5. Mada (Over Pride):

Not accepting the truth "I may go wrong." This happens to so many Traders and Investors. I have met many traders who are in the markets for 20 years and are still doing the same mistake they did 20 years ago. It's generally called **"Insanity: Repeating the same thing and expecting different results."** I have trained many Traders who have had more trading experience than that of my Age. They had accepted that there is a learning curve that is still left, so what is the Rama Trader's Secret Key for being a Trader?

"Always be a Student; never enact the role of a Professor."

- Accept your mistakes and the areas where you go wrong – which your 3 years' balance sheet of P&L will tell you – and seek for mentorship or Training.

Never consider yourself to be bigger than markets; the day you do, that is the day you could be said to be arrogant.

6. Matsara (Jealousy):

In System Trading and Investing, it might happen that your system would fail to work, while others' systems succeed, or when your stocks fail to perform, but other's stocks do. Under such circumstances, if you had religiously followed your system or had bought the stock consciously, then you should not feel insecure or jealous or shift to another system or stock, because, sooner or later, things would turn in your favor. Until that time, if the conviction is lost, you won't be having that stock or the system.

For e.g., If Mr. A. had invested in HUL from 2000 till 2008, Mr. A. would have only earned Dividend and nothing else, but only after that stock has given more than 200% Returns; the very same time, if he would have become jealous and invested in Infra, Real state Frenzy in 2007–08, the stock value would have been 70–80% down.

Only Jealousy of Knowledge should be entertained and not of the System or Stocks.

7. Swartha (Selfishness):

Many people advise me, not to share my trading secrets and I answer by saying that "There is no secret." It has been prevailing for centuries; I am only spreading & executing it. One holds a moral responsibility to share the knowledge and usher the correct path to others. That's probably the reason I have written this book, to share an insight on my journey.

In the same manner, out of the total trading or investment Income, there should be some percentage that should always be donated to make the world Beautiful!

8. Anyaaya (Injustice):

Injustice could be quoted as follows:

"The things where your capacity lies and you are unable to capitalize them."

For e.g.: We have a System or a Stock and we are confident that it can give a compounding of nearly 20% to 30% ROI for many years, but we invest only 3 to 5% of our total money, this is an injustice to both our Wealth and Knowledge.

Also, Injustice generally comes with knowing a lot of things and practicing nothing. I have seen so many intelligent people in markets possessing a meticulous knowledge, but when it comes to execution or Discipline, they fail to follow anything.

9. Amanavta (Cruelty):

Cruelty is a very strong word; it is tough to place it well as we are not intending to directly relate the human emotions here, but we are still CRUEL to ourselves in many ways: -

- If you know the stock you have bought is a mistake, and you must exit it; if you still don't do it, it's Cruelty to yourself.
- If you know the stock is doing great, and you book profit just to book some profits in your accounts, it is again Cruelty.
- Knowing what is right and wrong and still following the wrong route and thereafter repenting it is Cruelty.
- Not learning from the past mistakes and repeating them every time is Cruelty.

10. Ahankara (Ego):

Do you have the Best Trading System? Great. You have the best stocks with you? Great. Are you making huge money? Great, but along with all of these, if you have ego and arrogance, then things might fail to last for long.

I had this Giant ego of "I am never wrong" or "What I Predict always happens." The day I understood that it was my Ego, I kept it aside, and today I can claim that I am an Ego- Free Trader.

Ego kills a lot of Traders and Investors because of not learning and accepting the dynamics of the market.

As Maharatria always says, "From here where?" is a more profound thought than what you have already achieved in the past.

If one is able to put such characteristics to an end, then only one can proceed to become *212°: The Complete Trader*.

3 Action Steps to be taken from this Chapter:

1. Action Steps:

_____

_____

Date to Achieve it: _____

Accountable Person: _____

2. Action Steps:

_____

_____

Date to Achieve it: _____

Accountable Person: _____

3. Action Steps:

_____

_____

Date to Achieve it: _____

Accountable Person: _____

Notes:

_____

_____

_____

_____

_____

_____

_____

_____

Chapter 24

The Day of a 212°: The Complete Trader

"Show me your Schedule (Calendar) and I will show you where are you heading in your life."

A Trader's/Investor's Schedule is as important as a normal businessman's schedule, rather, I would say it is more important than any other businessmen's schedules in the world. Being a Trader/Investor, Discipline starts from the Time of waking up and ends at the time of sleeping. Discipline plays a major role in everything; it can't be the case that one is disciplined in his trading and not disciplined in his personal life.

After meeting, reading and practicing, I came up with one of the best schedules for a Full-Time Trader and Investor or what we generally call them – Traderpreneur. *212°: the complete Trader's* Schedule is not a Holy Grail Schedule; you can tweak it here and there, but its essence should remain the same.

Wake up between 4 and 4:30 – Get fresh for 30 minutes, make milk/coffee, or a smoothie. Write gratitude letter, and read something spiritual.

5 to 5: 30 – Do Meditation. Just sit with yourself in solitude, stop any thoughts coming into your mind and focus on your breath. This is the best time of the day; most of the best ideas will come at this point of time. Sit with pen and paper to jot down such ideas; they are majorly intuitions and are mostly right, also add up writing a Gratitude Book.

5.30 – 7:30 – Do any 2 Exercises you like – Running, Gym, workout, Swimming, Yoga, Tennis, etc. – which makes your heart beat to at least 160+.

7:30 to 8:30 – Family Time – spend time with your spouse, parents, and kids. Have fun and don't watch TV. Don't Miss to have **"Family Hug Time."**

9:00 to 9:45 – Wealth Work (Market Research) – Be it a Trader or Investor, one needs to focus on certain specific areas. I have 5 Technical Queries that I run every day; I review 500 Stock Charts every day, make a list of stocks to be bought or sold, and send them to my Execution department. This 45 minutes of focused work is the reason how my profits are going to be in the future.

I preferably believe in watching markets only twice –at the time of opening and closing, i.e., 30 minutes is the maximum time that one should invest in watching markets.

After market research, we have 6 blocks of 45 minutes; they should be ideally used as per one's working conditions such as:

- Reading Books/Listening to Audio Programs – Minimum blocks used for reading should be 3, i.e., minimum 135 minutes should be allotted for Reading
- Review of Risk Management
- Meeting Great, Intelligent Traders/Investors
- Watching Stock Market Movies

During the last 45 minutes of the day, Journalize your Trades and review markets, ensure adequate risk management.

Ask yourself **"Was I Disciplined today?"** and **"What can be done today to do better Tomorrow?"** and call it a day.

For a Trader, it's very important to have a balanced life; stop working post 1 hour of the market closure. In India, market closes at 3.30 p.m. I don't work after 4:47 p.m. I leave for home, and spend time with my spouse and kids, go for a walk, or watch TV or help my wife in her work etc.

Spend the last 45 minutes of your day to journalize your day and focus on reading your goals. It is said that the last 45 minutes you spend is generally what you manifest in your mind for the whole night and plan for the day ahead. So when you wake up tomorrow, you already have a planned day ahead.

Time to go to bed should not be later than 9 p.m. It is Mandatory for a Trader/Investor to have 7 Hours of Sleep; most of the work for Traders and Investors are governed through their minds. It has very less physical activity so the mind needs rest; sleep at the right time every day.

This is one of my favorite rituals; it's not necessary that you have the same schedule; you can surely design your own, but the following things are must in the schedule:

- Gratitude Book
- Meditation – Solitude
- Doing 2 Hours of Physical Activity
- Spending Most of the time with Family & Friends
- Focusing on Reading for at least 135 minutes a day
- Investing 45 minutes in reviewing your Craft – Uninterruptedly
- Planning for the 7–45 minutes Blocks you have in a day from 9 to 5
- Scanning the market only twice a day

- Journalizing your Trade after Markets
- Reviewing the goals and accordingly planning the day Ahead. It will uplift your position and make you the real 212°: The Complete Trader.

Summary & Learnings:

- A Fixed Daily Schedule is a must for a *212°: The Complete Trader*
- Waking up early is mandatory
- It's doing the boring thing that will make your successful
- Persistence is the key!

3 Action Steps to be taken from this Chapter:

1. Action Steps:

_____

_____

Date to Achieve it: _____

Accountable Person: _____

2. Action Steps:

_____

_____

Date to Achieve it: _____

Accountable Person: _____

3. Action Steps:

_____

_____

Date to Achieve it: _____

Accountable Person: _____

Notes:

_____
_____
_____
_____
_____
_____
_____
_____
_____

Chapter 25

Traderpreneur – Trading as a Real Business

"The business which makes money for you while you are asleep is the real business."

Traderpreneur is the word for Full-Time Traders and Investors. Trading is generally not considered as a full-time and serious business, but we believe at Turtle that being a Traderpreneur is one of the remarkable businesses on the earth.

I have been a business analyzer for more than a decade now, and through my personal experience, I have come to a conclusion that there is no business like Trading and Investing which possesses such level of competitive advantage. There is a competitive advantage in the form of benefits exceeding operational issues in comparison to other businesses.

I have been Professional Trader for a Quinquennial period – for the duration of 5 Years – and many more, and to be honest, I am not able to find any business which holds such a huge probability of turning an individual into a Millionaire. Information Technology is a business that has demonstrated a rapid flourishment in the last decade, but the futile ratio is much higher, and also, one needs to possess those exceptional skills and vision, which are rare to find. For people like us, with average acumen, being a Traderpreneur is one the best careers.

When I started my career, there were a very few Individuals who were Traderpreneurs in India. We could find more professional traders and investors only in Western Countries, but eventually, the approach changed and in today's date, even youth has realized its significance and started pursuing full-time trading as a career to enjoy it's fruitful returns.

Surat is the Diamond Capital of the World – nearly 90% of the Diamonds are produced in Surat and exported across the world. Initially, the Diamond Labourers were called "Ghasiyas" –the low caste people who polish Diamonds – and they were not seen with respect in the society. Today, they are called Diamond Engineers/Designers and they are bestowed with the utmost respect. Similar is the case with the Traders and Investors; today, a full-time trader or investor is called "Speculator" and is not seen with much respect in society, but I can claim it with surely, after a decade, he will be known as a lucky businessman who became a Traderpreneur. At Turtle Wealth, we do run an Agenda called #Tradingasabusiness, which we truly believe in, as the future lies in it!

Let us compare other businesses with a Full-Time Trading and Investing business.

Although, from the below mentioned comparisons, it can be clearly inferred that both the types of businesses are more or less similar in nature, yet there are certain significant advantages with being a Traderpreneur than being an ordinary entrepreneur.

Your Business/Self Employment	Traderpreneur
✓ Needs an Idea, Purpose & Passion	✓ Needs an Idea, Purpose and Passion
✓ Need Knowledge & Experience	✓ Need to Learn before doing it
✓ Needs an Initial Investment	✓ Needs initial investments
✓ Needs a Longevity Approach for 5 Years	✓ Trading also needs 5 years + to get real profits
✓ Need to take Calculated Risk	✓ Calculated risk is a must
✓ Takes Leverage of Opportunity	✓ Takes leverage of Opportunity
✓ Sometimes, Series of Month, Quarter, or even a Year can be in loss (in case of off season or crisis)	✓ If market is trendless, here also there could be loss "losses are the part of the business"
✓ There are Process & Systems	✓ In trading Systems and process, it is predefined
✓ Needs to Pay Income Tax	✓ Needs to pay income tax
✓ Needs to change as per trend	✓ Here too, change as per the market conditions and Trend is needed

8 Benefits of being a Traderpreneur:

1. Taking Short Position:

Now that is the benefit no other business on the earth holds. I have written about this in the previous chapters as well, yet it is one of the major benefits that are worth mentioning again. In every business, unfavorable conditions occur that leads to significant reduction in the demand, owing to the economic slowdown, or many other factors that influence the normal functioning of a business cycle. Under such circumstances, the ordinary businessmen become helpless and are only required to wait for a favorable situation. While, being a Traderpreneur, one can short the business and make substantial money by taking short position in it's the Index or Commodities. As a Full-Time Trader and Investor, no time is a bad time.

2. No Cost:

For any business, the 2 biggest costs are 1. Infrastructural Cost and 2. Man Power Cost. The most amazing part of being a **Traderpreneur** is that it accounts for the minimum cost in both areas. In the form of Infrastructure, a small office with 1–2 Computers in it, in the form of manpower, a handful of staff consisting of Executive Assistant, Dealer, etc. are required. With this much, one can trade for thousands, millions and even billions. If we take a small example of running a small-scale business with the mix of Infrastructural cost – rent, running expenses, other office expenses – and manpower cost, the total monthly expenditure would come to a minimum of 3–4 Lac, while being a **Traderpreneur,** this cost is cut down to as low as 50 to 80k a month. In normal business, till you earn 3–4 Lac, the breakeven point is not attained. While in Trading and Investing business, a loss of 3–4 lacs could be considered as the infrastructure cost of doing the business and this is its competitive advantage. If we understand that a loss of 3–4 lac a month is just an infrastructure cost while doing other business, but in Trading, that's the 1st Profit by simply being a **Traderpreneur**.

3. No Competition:

In all other businesses, competition leads to a major hit; the change in the pricing policy and other advancements are must for facing the dynamics of the competitions around. Nowadays, competition is not restricted to products; it has rather been expanded to Countries or technologies. Major revenue is steeled by the challenge of competition. Being a **Traderpreneur**, there is no such competition; it is just an Individual who is the competitor to himself. **"Here, one must beat himself every day, to grow from what he was yesterday."**

4. Invest or Trade in any Sector/Business/ World/Currency/Commodity:

If we are in any conventional business, it is very hard for us to come out of our cocoon and invest in other businesses. It requires a lot of understanding of other businesses accompanied by the requirement for a lot of funds. Whereas being a **Traderpreneur**, you can do it flawlessly. A year ago, I had the highest shareholding of NBFC Stocks in my portfolio, while after demonetization, I hold none of it. I rather have more shares of small technology companies now; I changed my strategies as per the market and as per the trend. In any other business, one is required to stay stuck to the industry and the commodities. Today I am Short 90% in Indian markets, but I am long in NASDAQ; I can trade across the countries, wherever I find strength. I take a long position and whenever the market weakens, I take a Short position.

5. 100% Transparency & Liquidity:

For any other business, the biggest challenge today is finding the buyers or sellers along with 100% transparency of the right price. It is the challenge in almost all the businesses, and it stands to be a significant challenge in case of SME business. Whereas being a **Traderpreneur**, we don't have to worry about the Buyer or Seller. The price is 100% transparent for anyone trading from any part of the world at a time, and that second the price will remain the same and equal for everyone, irrespective of the quantity of investment. In any other business, most of the time goes in the negotiation of the prices and finding the right buyer and the right seller; this again proves to be the biggest advantage of being a **Traderpreneur.**

6. No Bad Debts:

In almost every business, the major problem today is a cycle of payment, which is majorly of 30, 60 and even 90 days, and only after that, the bills are recovered and profits are retained. So, after 5 years the owner forgets creativity, and innovations and his major focus are laid only on clearing the pending payments. Gradually, this impacts the business and it goes down, whereas in Trading and

Investing, the credit payment is never an issue. If you make profits, it is guaranteed that the money will be credited to the account on the same day or maximum by the next working day. Just think, in other businesses, forget profits, if the opposite party goes bankrupt, the recovery of even the principal amount gets exposed to risk. While being a **Traderpreneur,** the probability of counterparty risk is near to 0.

7. Scale up:

Today, if a businessman wants to scale up the business with supposedly 10 new branches or showrooms, it has to go through numerous big hurdles of Infrastructure, employees, systems, demand, etc., whereas a **Traderpreneur** can scale up anytime – the only requirement is the right level of understanding the leverage and risk management. This business gives you such a level of free leverage that is not available in any business, and this is how one can scale up without any kind of infrastructure or manpower requirements. If you put this cost wisely, it delivers a profitability ratio of 5 times & more.

8. Living Life:

Let me ask a Question. Why do we do business or job – any business?

The answer is financial security, for ourselves and our family. But who are the unhappy people around us? They are either us or our family. As we are so much indulged in the business, we hardly have any time for ourselves, our family, health, and society. In the end, we have lost the great moments of our lives, childhood of kids, health, time for learning and communicating. This happens with almost everyone, who are into business, but the life of a Traderpreneur is different; he has sufficient time for Health, Society and Family. Still, he is into the best business of the lifetime. I personally take so many vacations; I work very less in terms of number of hours; I give ample amount of time to Health, Family and Friends; still, I have spare time to read books and communicate with great people.

One of the most respected people in the Diamond Industry of Surat – Mr. Parag Shah told me, **"We have to differentiate the things that are Priceless with the things which could be bought with a Price."** Priceless things such as Great Health, Family and fun with Daughter/Son, can never be bought with money. Being a Traderpreneur, you can have both in life – **"Things which are priceless, and things which can be bought with a Price."**

Summary & Learnings:

- To be a Traderpreneur is honourable
- Trading & Investing is the best business where one can enjoy life
- It has more benefits than any other conventional business

3 Action Steps to be taken from this Chapter:

1. Action Steps:

_____

_____

Date to Achieve it: _____

Accountable Person: _____

2. Action Steps:

_____

_____

Date to Achieve it: _____

Accountable Person: _____

3. Action Steps:

_____

_____

Date to Achieve it: _____

Accountable Person: _____

Notes:

_____

_____

_____

_____

_____

_____

_____

_____

Chapter 26

The EPW Model

As a full-time trader/investor, I have always been worried about my survival in the world and the society, as there persists a widely-accepted rational that the long-term survival of a full-time trader is hardly possible. Yet, in my journey as a trader/investor and an entrepreneur, I have made a model through which, I believe, I am on my right track to be a billionaire.

We generally give tags to our self as a Trader or Investor such as:

- I am a Technical Trader
- I am a Fundamental Investor
- I am a System Trader
- I am a Swing Trader
- I am Discretion Trader
- I am a Value Investor
- I am a Newsterian Trader – the one who trades on news
- I am an Option Trader

And this never-ending list goes on and on. In my journey as a trader and investor, I have found that a successful trader is expected to do everything including trading, investing, options, value investing and many more, that results in **"Unlimited Profits and Limited Losses."** But, what could be

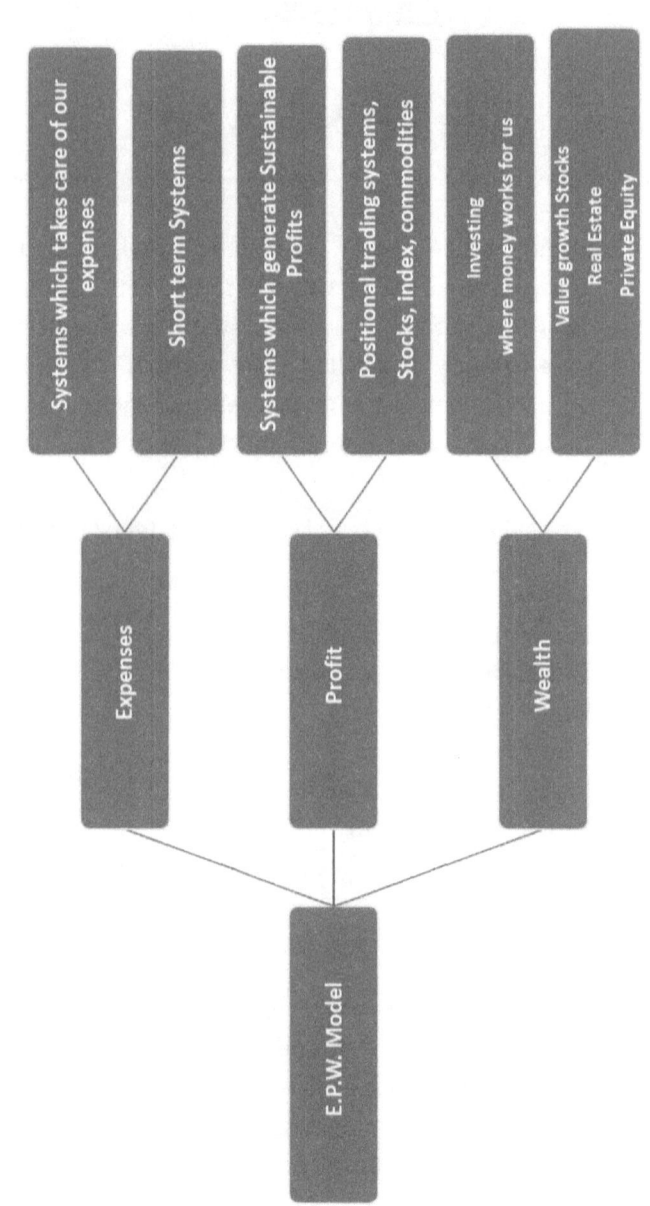

the perfect model for attaining such a result? The answer to this question is EPW Model that has been depicted through the above-mentioned flow chart.

E = Expenses Module: As a Human following are most common expenses that are to be taken care of:

- Living Expenses
- Food
- Kids' Education
- Vacations
- General Expenses
- Loans etc.

We need to make a system that makes our expenses organized and structured. With this system in place, you can relax and take a backseat while the expenses are automatically managed.

Let us assume that Mrs. C. has an expense of 60,000 INR per Month –1000$ – she makes a system that is short-term on index or options, she gives time to backtest it, with limited exposure and risk, she can easily achieve 60,000 INR in a month. In the initial months, she must take care of trades; after a quarter, she could delegate this task to a dealer, after which she can be totally relaxed that her monthly expenses are being automatically looked after.

When I understood this, I designed a short-term system on stocks and delegated it to my wife Namrata; she is a homemaker and takes care of our lovely daughter; she wanted a profession that could be done from home, and nothing could be more convenient and substantial than being a full-time trader.

Today, she takes care of the whole house, settles all the expenses and whatever we save after the above-stated expenses, we divert its flow for financing our holidays and other luxuries. Irony is that she is not that much aware of systems and markets, but she trades as per systems without even applying her brains. Most of the times, she does not know what company is she trading in and what business does it do, and that is the beauty of being a trader – just following the price; leaving everything aside.

So, when you have an expenses system, your profit area won't be disturbed and you won't have any extra pressure to handle the expenses.

P = Profit = Cash Flow

For a trader/investor, generally, profits are affected by the expenses– the higher the profits, the higher the expenses and an urge to buy ultra-luxury liabilities like Car, Home, Clubhouse membership, expensive holidays, etc. also rise.

In my initial years, after learning the strategy through which Mr. Rakesh Jhunjhunwala made a massive wealth, I understood that one should trade and ensure a regular cash flow and the same cash flow should be invested in brilliant assets, but my expenses were taking a toll on my wealth and profit zone.

So now when my expenses are taken care of, profits only flow in generating further income and it could add up to the wealth division.

We at Turtle have designed systems in index, options & commodities which are quite moderate – as per our Personalities – and give a decent return similar to other business returns, which hold less tracking, fewer trades and moderate drawdowns. However, my exposure is much higher towards my personal expenses.

Profits are the most important segment of the EPW model as it is the source through which wealth could be augmented. Once when I met Mr. Buffett, I understood that his primary secret of wealth was not only his style of picking stocks; it was rather Berkshire Hathaway which gave him nearly 50 Billion dollars to invest. Just imagine what a massive amount of cash flow he must have created from the Insurance business. Same is the case with almost all the billionaire traders and Investors; they have an area of consistent cash flow and that is one of their secrets of making massive wealth.

Profit segment is traded in an area of positional to Long-Term Trading/Investment. I Trade in the Stocks, Index and Commodities in P = Profit Accounts.

Wealth:

Without wealth, we cannot grow bigger, and this is only possible if the profit is shifted to wealth; both the things are correlated to each other.

I tend to buy long-term wealth creating stocks that have consumption model where the products of the company will be used even if the world goes into recession, such as Gillette, P&G, Dabur, Pididlite, Google, Maruti, etc.

These stocks are not my buying recommendations – How to pick stocks is one of the chapters in the book. I also invest in Mid Cap ETFs, which are generally very less volatile compared to other stocks and investments. However, these stocks are liquid and could be used in trading margins as well, which could again boost the profit segments. Inspired by the Investing process of Mr. Utpal Sheth (CEO-Rare), I advise segregating the Wealth in 3 Asset Classes.

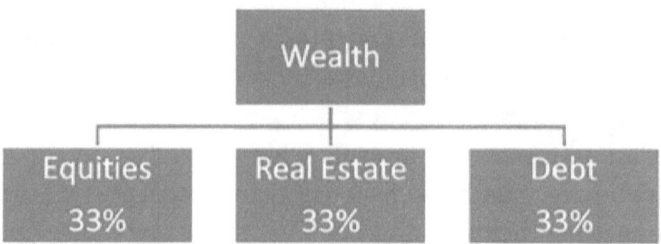

All the assets will face their boom and bust times; moreover, they will counter one another. Equities will give higher returns in a bull period when the respective invested companies will consistently perform and dividend can be said to be a passive income; real estate holds a good yield on rental incomes in commercial property – also a passive income – and provides sustainable wealth for a longer period.

The Debt being the investment with a passive income of fixed interest earnings, it would not seem to be attractive at all, but would work wonders when the other 2 investments fail to provide requisite returns.

The idea is that we are already taking a high level of risk in E & P area, and so in the wealth segment, our risk should be diversified into 3 asset classes which eventually grow with the passage of time by providing higher and higher passive Income.

As a **212°: *The complete Trader***, we should be having a quest of making a diversified profit generating system in major asset class to be shifted to the wealth segment.

EPW Model	Expenses	Profits	Wealth
Systems	Short Term - Daily or Weekly	Medium Term to Long Term	Long Term Wealth Creation
Risk	High to Moderate	Moderate	Low
Leverage	High Leverage	Calculated Leverage	No Leverage
Objective	To take out Monthly Expenses	To generate Profits & sustainable Cash flow	To Invest in assets that can give Passive income with Long Term Wealth Generation
Return Expectations	High to Moderate	Moderate	Low
Diversification Ratio	Low	Low to Mix	High (In different asset class)
Risk Taking Objective	Moderate	Moderate	Moderate to Low

The above table explains how exactly the EPW model works and can prove to be the technique of changing yourself from a trader to the *212°: The Complete Trader.*

Summary & Learnings:
- Segregation of Expenses with the Profits is a must
- Profits should be re-invested and compounded in Wealth Area
- EPW model Should be followed with a high level of Discipline

3 Action Steps to be taken from this Chapter:

1. Action Steps:

_____

_____

Date to Achieve it: _____

Accountable Person: _____

2. Action Steps:

_____

_____

Date to Achieve it: _____

Accountable Person: _____

3. Action Steps:

_____

_____

Date to Achieve it: _____

Accountable Person: _____

Notes:

Chapter 27

12 Learnings for Being a 212° Trader/Investor

"The one who is stronger is 5 minutes more strong than one who is not." – Anonymous

Every day in life, being Traders and Investors, we learn something new. I have listed my 12 lessons of the lifetime that would enlighten one's knowledge on stocks.

1. No Stock is too cheap to Short & No Stock is too expensive to buy:

While taking a short position in a stock, you should never think that this is a stock which is too less in price to go down further, or when you long a stock, you should not think that the stock has gone too high; that should not be the reason to take a long position. It's all about percentage; we have also taken a short position in a stock which was in single digit and earned 30%, and we have taken a long position in a stock which was 30,000 rupees and earned 60% – mass won't do this – so there remains a fair probability of getting more returns. I have a system where if the stock crosses a new decimal for the first time, i.e., 10, 100, 1,000 or 10,000, it's the best time to long that stock, or if the stock breaks the 1st decimal, it's a great time to short that stock.

2. The Trades which you expect the least would give you the best returns:

It has happened numerous times and it will keep happening. Howsoever we try to be emotionless, our emotions are linked with the positions. When I expected too much from a stock, it never gave me returns, and when I least expected from a trade, it turned out to be the most profitable trade of my life. It happens in markets as well. Where there is the highest expectation of returns, the market never delivers returns, and we fear about an investment or a trade, it's returns turn out to be phenomenal. Our emotions should be like the old weighing machines that used to be available in the grocery store; the indicator must attain perfect balance, i.e., the pointer should stay in the center of the scale to ensure the desired level of emotions that one should carry in every Trade/Investment.

3. Returns are not generated from where crowd invests:

Over the period, in every asset class, I have marked one thing

"Where there is a mass investment, one won't find returns." Most of the investment decisions are taken based on the fact that-if everybody is investing, we would also invest. It's a sheep mentality to walk in herds, but sheep are generally slaughtered. Find your own niche and system of Investing in any asset class as per your wisdom, not as per the crowd.

4. Peace of mind is very important:

One thing that very few people talk about is the peace of mind; your position should not reflect your emotions, whether it is profit or loss, it shouldn't matter. One should get good sleep at night. If the Dow Jones is 500 points up or down and still remains favorable then wealth is sure in one's way.

5. Shreya and Preya:

This comes from Katha Upanishads, Shreya is where one takes "Short-Term Pain for Long-Term Benefits" and Preya is "Short-Term pleasure but long-term Pain." It is similar to the scenario, where one undergoes a trade and books profits just to earn that extra buck. It is pleasure in short term but if that stock or position doesn't go the right way, its surely a pain. In the same way, if one earns exceptionally well in a Financial Year, and with that money, he compounds and avoids to use liability, it is a pain for short term but pleasure for Long Term. My learning has been to ask myself every time, "Are we doing 'Shreya' or 'Preya?'" Also, "Shrey" is the honor given to the person who follows the path of "Shreya."

6. Where I will die:

In the Must-Read book "Poor Charlie's Almanack," Mr. Charlie Munger has stated that one has to find out "Where will one die?" and has to stay consistently vigilant so that one doesn't die. I follow this thought religiously. Every Monday, at 11:30 A.M., Turtle Team sits for 45 minutes to discuss "Where will we die?" The thought is to find a Black Swan, to review the positions, to review what if the market goes 10% downside tomorrow; are we prepared? What if we need some extra funds tomorrow; are we prepared? There are hundreds of analogies that we think and take steps accordingly.

We are Professional Traders/Investors, so we do it every week. One can do it Monthly/Quarterly, but asking this question, again and again, is very important. When we make a system or execute a system, the 1st question we should ask ourselves is "Where is the death hidden?" It means that it could be a part of the system that might kill us, and went unnoticed. Repeatedly asking such questions can make the system and confidence robust.

7. A good time is a bad time and a bad time is a good time:

In the journey, we will pass through both Good as well as Bad times for sure, but mark my words, the reason for bad times is always because of our good times, and the reason for good times is because of our bad times.

The lessons that we learn in bad times and act on would improve our decisions and makes us better and even best. But again, in that time we get overconfident and do over leverage, with the thinking that I cannot go wrong, and I am bigger than markets. We take our good time for granted, to get bad times; In Good times, I would advise you to be extremely humble, not to spend too much, take the tough decisions, save enough and Invest time in relations. This probably will never give you bad times, and if one still gets it, it would be a big jump coming on the way.

8. The Secret is Power of Compounding:

The power of compounding is taught in 3rd Standard but we hardly follow it. Everything in life depends on compounding one's health, Money, Relationship, etc. Mass believes that Compounding works only in Investing, not in Trading, but both have a common aim – to earn money. The art of being wealthy and the route of becoming a billionaire and millionaire is only through the way of Compounding. When I understood earning 15% return for 30 years is not 450% return but it is 6500% return, My complete focus got shifted from daily or monthly return targets to compound it yearly. It takes enormous sacrifice, hard work, conviction and patience to compound wealth. The power of compounding wealth will only be beneficial if one compounds its health first. Let us take an example, 99% of Mr. Warren Buffett's wealth was made after he turned 50. If Mr. Warren Buffett had died at the age of 55, probably half of the world would not have known who Mr. Warren Buffett was, as his age was on his side, the compounding of Wealth worked. So it is always health first and then wealth.

9. Invest in Knowledge First:

None of my paternal or maternal family had been into the stock markets. Whatever I had learned was by meeting people and reading great books. The only way to grow is to have an association with great people, read fantastic books and take superb vacations – these 3 habits will build a World-class Trader & Investor.

10. Investing and Trading:

As per my Learning, allocation of both Investments and Trading is the essential aspect to be ensured; it is very hard to grow only as a Trader or only as an Investor; one should have a mix of 2 brains. Investing is wealth creation and trading is cash flow creation for creating wealth.

11. Values & Integrity are more important than Money:

I have always given relatively more importance to values than money. Values cannot be taken back; money can be earned again. I have always given my team more than they had asked for. If there lies a problem because of money, I will sacrifice money over relation or over some other issues, as value is like sleep and money is like a dream, you need sleep before getting good dreams.

12. Never Retire:

These days, all insurance companies offer numerous retirement plans. Many of my friends say that they want to get retired by 40–45 years of age. I get shocked. Why would you want to retire from what you love? So, I advise my friends, "Don't retire at 40–45; you should rather retire right now, as you don't love what you are doing." I am going to live for 108 years, and till my last breath, I would be talking about trading, Investing and Business; that's my love for this business and that's the reason retirement is not made for me, as one realizes the epitome of wealth and success only after he turns 60, it's the compounding of Wealth, Wisdom and Wife's Advise that you are working on.

3 Action Steps to be taken from this Chapter:

1. Action Steps:

_____

_____

Date to Achieve it: _____

Accountable Person: _____

2. Action Steps:

_____

_____

Date to Achieve it: _____

Accountable Person: _____

3. Action Steps:

_____

_____

Date to Achieve it: _____

Accountable Person: _____

Notes:

_____

_____

_____

_____

_____

_____

_____

_____

Chapter 28

21 Things I Wished to Have Known before I Started Trading/Investing

1. Investing in Knowledge is the first Investment to be done before investing in markets
2. Reading 100 Pages of any Trading/Investing book every day would have saved me from a lot of mistakes
3. Unlimited Profits and Limited Losses – Big Profits and Small Losses – is the only way to succeed in the markets
4. The lesser lure you have towards profits, the more you attain them
5. The ones who have the habit of giving, the Universe gives more to them; on the contrary, the ones who have the habit of taking, the universe takes from them
6. Health is one of the core reasons to be successful as a trader or investor
7. Association with sharp minds is more valuable than any insider information or Strategy
8. Backtesting is like the backbone of a Trader/Investor
9. If one is confident on a thesis or a system, betting small is a sin; in the same way, betting high on a system or thesis which is not logical is a bigger Sin!
10. Having a Trading/Investing Buddy is very important, especially during the tough times

11. Everyone has a unique style of Trading/Investing; no one can copy the style of the other; to be the best, we must make our own style of investing and Trading as per our personality
12. Money Management is the key to survival – Pyramiding in Investing and applying Martingale theory in Trend Following is the Holy Grail
13. Until any unavoidable circumstances, do not exit till the Happy Loss is triggered, and once it is triggered, don't think of anything else
14. You can't be only a Trader or an Investor; you have to be everything to make money, and once you achieve that stage, you can have choices of what you like and what you don't
15. There are 2 sides to everything except wisdom; nothing is precisely right and precisely wrong in the markets
16. One can't compare himself to the ones who have made a lot of money like Mr. Warren Buffet, Mr. Rakesh Jhunjhunwala, etc.; they had their own share of battles to fight, and their battles could be different from those of ours
17. Even the God has failed in keeping everyone happy; hence, it's impossible for an individual to keep everyone happy
18. Compounding is the only way to make it big and bigger; there is no other way around
19. Waking up early is the 1st step to get the Success
20. Take more vacations, especially alone
21. Run your own race. Focus on your goals, and God will bring the right people into your life

Chapter 29

The KIDS Approach

"You don't need another computer, another screen, a faster internet connection, etc. You have all you need between your ears. Develop it."

I hope the above chapters have assisted you in adding up to your thought process, and you might have gained clear understanding to proceed in the process of becoming *212°: The Complete Trader*, but everything is in vain if we failed to implement it practically and an adequate action plan is not in place.

A few years ago, through a management book, I learnt about the exercise named KIDS and I found it to be more practical and effective in comparison to the other self-analytical exercises such as SWOT. Through this exercise, thousands of traders have been able to change their behavior and habits.

KEEP: Whatever Is Going Well, Keep Continuing It

This section contains the attributes that you already perceive as your strengths and would like to maintain them as your edge over others.

For example: Being Passionate about trading; attaining continuous knowledge, the right attitude, trading as a business, etc.

IMPROVE: Identify the weak areas, to convert them into your strengths

This section contains your attributes that can be called as your weaknesses and enhancing it will lead to improved productivity and your trading performance would rise to a very high level.

For example: Skills of being Trader, Health, Trading and Investing; Skills to do short.

DEVELOP: Identify the attributes that you require in order to improve or stay competitive

This section contains the attributes that are yet to be explored, such as trading knowledge, new markets, better mental state, better health, better connections, etc.

STOP/SCRAP: Activities that are not adding value and are rather wasting your time and depreciating your trading performance

For example: Negative thinking, watching TV, seeking tips, non-adherence of rule-regulations in trading etc.

Exercise:

KEEP: Whatever is going well, keep continuing it

1. _____
2. _____
3. _____
4. _____
5. _____

IMPROVE: Identify the weak areas, to convert them into your strengths

1. _____
2. _____
3. _____
4. _____
5. _____

DEVELOP: Identify the attributes that you need in order to improve or stay competitive

1. _____
2. _____
3. _____
4. _____
5. _____

STOP: Identify the activities that are not adding value and are rather wasting your time and depreciating your trading performance

1. _____
2. _____
3. _____
4. _____
5. _____

I am sure at the end of this chapter, your thought process will be changed. Review the 1st Survey given at the beginning of the book again, and take the review. The answer should come as 10 out of 10. If you have not achieved that score yet, read more.

Take a deep breath, because the journey has just begun...

References:

1. Parker, S. 2005. 212: The Extra Degree. WalkTheTalk.com.
2. NSE india equities. 2014. [online]. Available at: https://www.nse-india.com/products/content/equities/equities/equities.htm. [Assessed on 09 March 2015].

www.ingramcontent.com/pod-product-compliance
Lightning Source LLC
Chambersburg PA
CBHW020638220526
45464CB00001B/203